CHRIS SLOANE

Online Marketing For Paving Companies

HEAVISIDE

First published by Heaviside Group 2022

Second edition

ISBN: 978-1-7353136-2-7

This book was professionally typeset on Reedsy.
Find out more at reedsy.com

Contents

1

Introduction

Thanks for reading our new and revised book, Online Marketing For Paving Companies!

In this guide we will walk you through the important things you need to do to establish an effective online presence and explain:

- How the search engines work and what you need to do to handle each part of them for maximum visibility and return.
- How the map listings work and how to get your paving company listed on the map.
- Our search engine optimization strategy for paving companies.
- Our social media strategy specifically for paving companies.
- Our paid search strategy designed to be effective for paving companies.

I am excited to be sharing this information with you. There are tons of information sources out there from lots of so-called experts, but it can be very hard to tell what is good information and what is not.

What I'm going to talk about in this book is based on our work with dozens of paving companies just like yours over the past few years.

We know what works because we've done it, and I'm going to show you exactly what to do.

"We were really hesitant to change marketing companies but Paving Marketers has exceeded our expectations. We have been more busy than we've been in years, the calls are much better quality than we used to get, and they have been hard to keep up with!"
- Joni Seyko, JR Paving & Construction Co

Who Are These Guys?

Before getting too deep here I would like to introduce myself.

My name is Chris Sloane. I am the founder of Paving Marketers. I have been working in SEO, web development, and digital marketing for over 10 years.

In 2011 I founded Heaviside Group, which grew over time

to one of the top marketing agencies in the Midwest, with locations in Waukesha, WI and Cincinnati, OH and over **five hundred** five-star reviews. Heaviside has worked with over 1,000 clients all around the world, spanning all six inhabited continents. If I could sell SEO to penguins it would be all seven.

My background prior to that was in physics – and while it may seem unrelated, the process of breaking something down to find out why and how it works is very relevant to this profession. Unlike physics, the rules are constantly changing as the search engine algorithms evolve. What worked well a year ago is often not quite the same today.

I have worked with international enterprises to SaaS companies to small retail storefronts. While I cannot say we have seen it all, I can say we have seen enough!

Everything I will be talking about here has been learned "in the trenches" on real projects that helped grow leads and sales for businesses of all types.

What We Do

Spoiler alert: our company does this stuff. My team has built websites, attracted search engine traffic, driven profitable paid visitors, increased conversion rates with retargeting, and on and on.

We have a proven process designed to triple your sales by

getting your internet marketing right. That process is what this book is based on.

We would love the opportunity to work with you and do this for your business. But that is not what this book is – it is not going to be a hidden sales presentation that is going to require you to buy services from us to *really* make things work.

I want to give you the best information out there on how to do this stuff for your own business. If you take this information and implement the process, it is going to work for you, and you are going to succeed.

Thanks again for checking out our book!

Chris Sloane
Founder, Paving Marketers

About Paving Marketers

PAVING MARKETERS

Based in Waukesha, Wisconsin with clients throughout the United States, Paving Marketers was founded by Chris Sloane. Our mission is to help 300 paving companies dominate their market and triple their sales.

We strive for excellence in everything we do; from the websites we design and engineer, to the results we deliver, to the customer service our clients receive. Our proven solutions are built on 10+ years of marketing experience.

With Paving Marketers, you get paving industry expertise, proven strategies, market exclusivity, complete transparency, and unmatched support.

Proud member of the National Asphalt Paving Association.

About You

What do we know about you? Obviously we don't know who you are, but we know who is interested in what we do.

We've learned a lot from talking to paving/concrete companies. Each one is different, but the people we talk to generally have this in common:

1. They know marketing on the internet is important, and they want to get more (or LOTS more) inbound leads for commercial jobs. Quality residential jobs too!
2. They have been burned before and want to work with

someone who knows the industry and can deliver results.

If the first one applies to you, you're going to love this book.

If the second one applies to you, you're also going to love this book. Then, once you are done reading it you're going to want to go to https://pavingmarketers.com/apply-now and set up a call to talk to us about how we can do this for you.

We focus on helping our clients get leads from people searching online for paving companies. At the end of June in 2022, I looked at all of the 1342 leads that came in for our paving clients and broke down where they came from:

- 33.6% from Google Ads
- 36.9% from Google Maps
- 20.1% from Google Organic
- 9.4% from Other
- Mostly direct, could be any of the other three
- Yahoo and Bing almost nothing

Keep this in mind as you read this book, so that you can understand where you should prioritize your efforts.

Before we get started, let me show you some client results. Some are spending a lot on ad spend, some are not. Some are getting huge results from maps and some are still in progress. I want to show you a range of possible outcomes here – but mostly that the results from the things we talk about are real.

Results

Here are some examples from June 2022. These are the raw lead totals, unfiltered. Some are going to be not quotable, some are duplicates, a few would be repeat customers from before. But all of these clients are seeing enough activity from online searches to create estimates and book jobs for their crew(s) to produce.

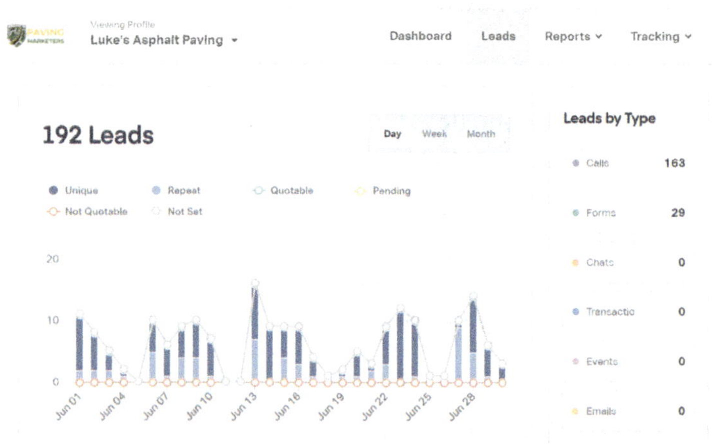

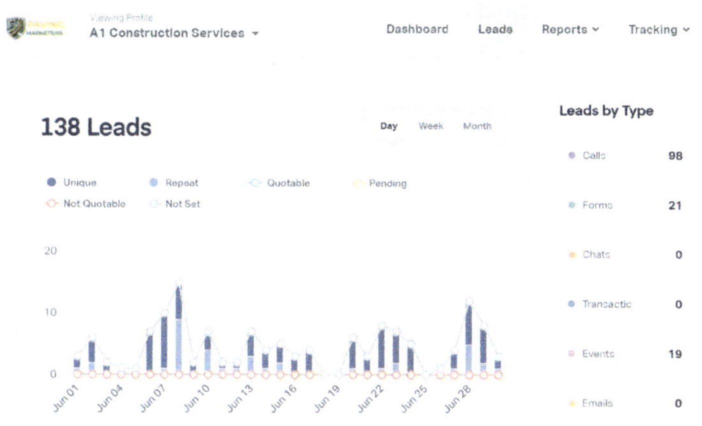
Viewing Profile
A1 Construction Services
Dashboard
Leads
Reports
Tracking
138 Leads
Day
Week
Month
Unique
Repeat
Quotable
Pending
Not Quotable
Not Set
20
10
0
Jun 01
Jun 04
Jun 07
Jun 10
Jun 13
Jun 16
Jun 19
Jun 22
Jun 25
Jun 28
Leads by Type
Calls 98
Forms 21
Chats 0
Transactic 0
Events 19
Emails 0

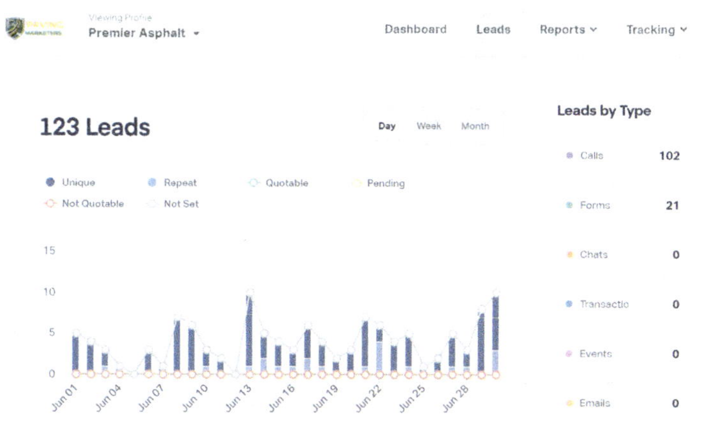
Viewing Profile
Premier Asphalt
Dashboard
Leads
Reports
Tracking
123 Leads
Day
Week
Month
Unique
Repeat
Quotable
Pending
Not Quotable
Not Set
15
10
5
0
Jun 01
Jun 04
Jun 07
Jun 10
Jun 13
Jun 16
Jun 19
Jun 22
Jun 25
Jun 28
Leads by Type
Calls 102
Forms 21
Chats 0
Transactio 0
Events 0
Emails 0

Viewing Profile
JR Paving & Construction
Dashboard
Leads
Reports
Tracking
115 Leads
Day
Week
Month
Unique
Repeat
Quotable
Pending
Not Quotable
Not Set
15
10
5
0
Jun 01
Jun 04
Jun 07
Jun 10
Jun 13
Jun 16
Jun 19
Jun 22
Jun 25
Jun 28
Leads by Type
Calls 88
Forms 27
Chats 0
Transactio 0
Events 0
Emails 0

Viewing Profile
Boston Choice Driveways
Dashboard
Leads
Reports
Tracking
78 Leads
Day
Week
Month
Unique
Repeat
Quotable
Pending
Not Quotable
Not Set
15
10
5
0
Jun 01
Jun 04
Jun 07
Jun 10
Jun 13
Jun 16
Jun 19
Jun 22
Jun 25
Jun 28
Leads by Type
Calls 68
Forms 10
Chats 0
Transactio 0
Events 0
Emails 0

Viewing Profile
Biondi Paving
Dashboard
Leads
Reports
Tracking
76 Leads
Day
Week
Month
Unique
Repeat
Quotable
Pending
Not Quotable
Not Set
10
5
0
Jun 01
Jun 04
Jun 07
Jun 10
Jun 13
Jun 16
Jun 19
Jun 22
Jun 25
Jun 28
Leads by Type
Calls 61
Forms 10
Chats 0
Transactio 0
Events 5
Emails 0

Viewing Profile
Yeghoian Grading & Paving
Dashboard
Leads
Reports
Tracking
68 Leads
Day
Week
Month
Unique
Repeat
Quotable
Pending
Not Quotable
Not Set
10
5
0
Jun 01
Jun 04
Jun 07
Jun 10
Jun 13
Jun 16
Jun 19
Jun 22
Jun 25
Jun 28
Leads by Type
Calls 61
Forms 7
Chats 0
Transactio 0
Events 0
Emails 0

Viewing Profile
Bluff City Paving
Dashboard
Leads
Reports
Tracking
65 Leads
Day
Week
Month
Unique
Repeat
Quotable
Pending
Not Quotable
Not Set
10
5
0
Jun 01
Jun 04
Jun 07
Jun 10
Jun 13
Jun 16
Jun 19
Jun 22
Jun 25
Jun 28
Leads by Type
Calls 54
Forms 11
Chats 0
Transactio 0
Events 0
Emails 0

Viewing Profile
American Asphalt Sealing ...
Dashboard
Leads
Reports
Tracking
61 Leads
Day
Week
Month
Unique
Repeat
Quotable
Pending
Not Quotable
Not Set
10
5
0
Jun 01
Jun 04
Jun 07
Jun 10
Jun 13
Jun 16
Jun 19
Jun 22
Jun 25
Jun 28
Leads by Type
Calls 60
Forms 1
Chats 0
Transactio 0
Events 0
Emails 0

2

Understanding Online Marketing Channels

When it comes to Internet marketing for your paving business, there are several avenues to explore. In this chapter, we will briefly touch on the various Internet marketing channels that are available, and then go into more detail throughout the book.

If you tried to come up with a list of places you could advertise online, it would probably look something like this:

1. Search Engine Optimization (Organic Listings and Map Listings)
2. Search Engine Marketing/PPC on Google Ads and Bing Search Network
3. Social Media Marketing (Facebook, Twitter, LinkedIn)
4. Video Marketing
5. Email Marketing
6. Paid Lead Services (HomeAdvisor, Angi, Networx, etc)

Let's talk about each one of these in a bit more detail.

Search Engine Optimization

Search Engine Optimization (SEO) is the process of increasing your paving company's visibility on major search engines (Google, Yahoo, Bing, etc.) in the organic, non-paid listings as consumers are searching for someone to pave their driveway or restripe their parking lot..

There are three very critical components of Search Engine Marketing. The three components are: Paid (or Ads), Organic, and Maps.

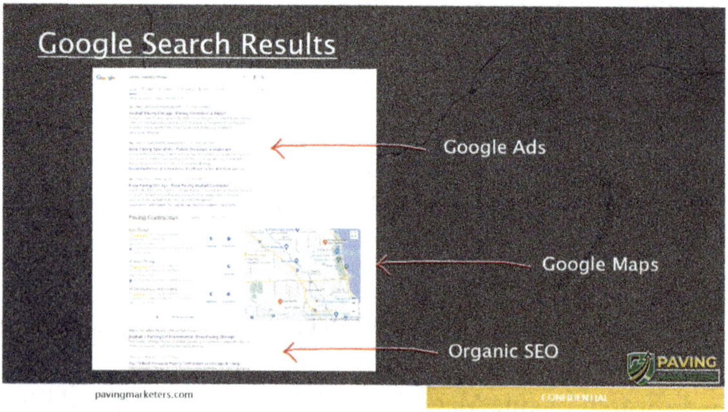

Let's look more closely at each one. We'll go into more detail in the next chapter but I'd like to introduce them here.

Paid Listings

The area along the top and side that advertisers can bid on and pay for in order to obtain decent placement in the search engines.

We watch these across the US for paving companies, and in almost every single market there are tons of advertisers. These are typically a mix of paid lead companies (HomeAdvisor, Angi, etc) and real paving companies competing for the leads.

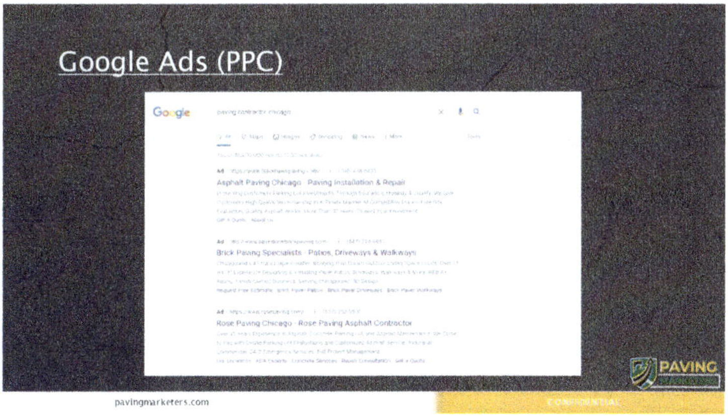

Organic Listings

The area in the body of the Search Engine Results page. When you get 5 emails a day selling you "SEO" – this is what they are talking about.

This is what is typically thought of as "SEO" and when you're tracking how you're doing for "parking lot paving company" this is probably what you're looking at.

Map Listings

These are the listings which come up beneath the paid listings and above the organic listings in a number of searches. This is the second most important source of leads! Don't overlook it.

Think about how you search for a restaurant, or plumber. Your customers search for you the same way.

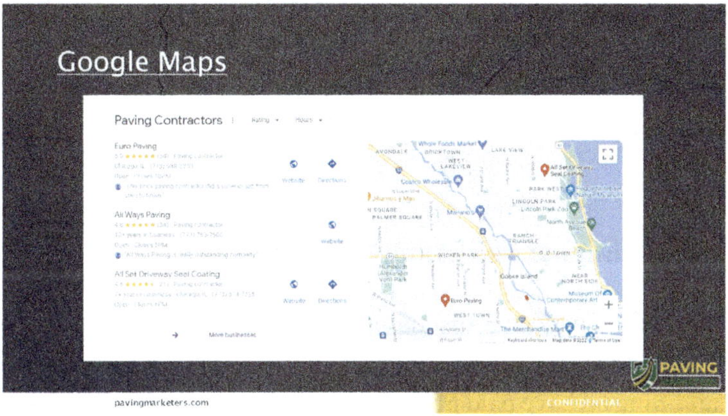

Search Engine Optimization involves getting your website to show up in the Organic and Map Listings. These listings account for a majority of the search volume. As depicted in the illustration below, more than 78% of searchers click on the Organic (non-paid listings) rather than the paid listings.

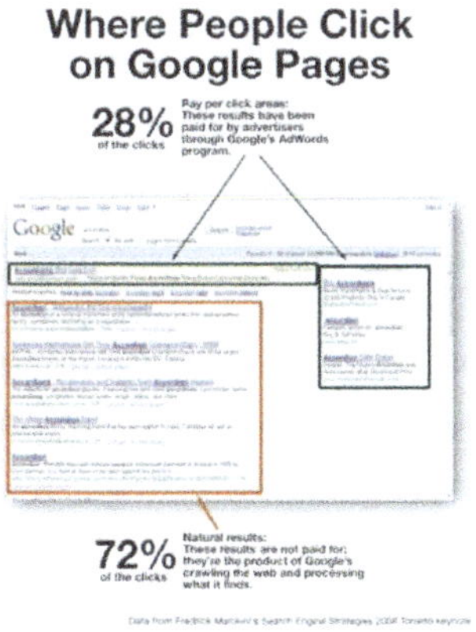

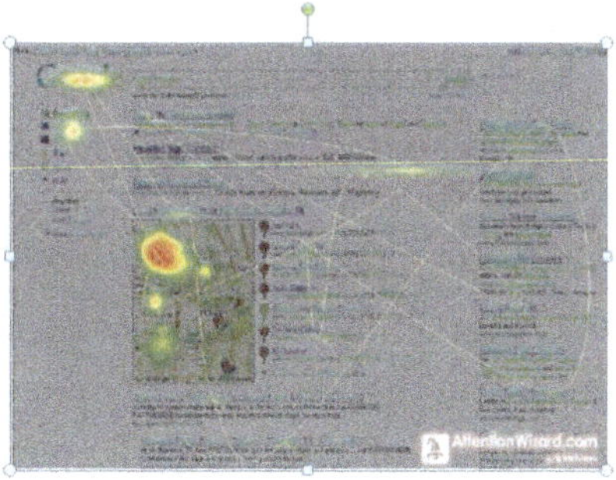

When most people think "Internet Marketing," they think Search Engine Optimization. However, you will begin to see that SEO is only a small piece of the MUCH BIGGER "Internet Marketing" puzzle for paving companies.

Search Engine Marketing / Pay-Per-Click

Now that we have discussed SEO, let's talk about Search Engine Marketing or PPC (Pay-Per-Click). Google, Yahoo and Bing all have paid programs that allow you to BUY listings associated with your keywords to be placed in designated areas of their sites.

There are three really important benefits of PPC:

1. Your keyword listings will appear on search engines almost immediately
2. You only have to pay when someone actually clicks on your listing – hence the term Pay-Per-Click Marketing
3. You can get your ad to show up on national terms in the areas/cities in which you operate

PPC Marketing works on an auction system similar to that of eBay. You simply choose your keywords and propose a bid of what you would be willing to pay for each click.

There are several factors that determine placement which will be discussed in detail in the Google Ads chapter. But, in the broadest sense, the one who is willing to pay the most per click will be rewarded the top position in the search engines, while the second-most will be in the second position, etc.

BUT – Google cares about what it's own customers see (i.e. the searchers) and they will reward you for having a high-quality ad, and landing page. So if you know what you are doing, you can pay less per click than the other guys and still get the top spot.

PPC Marketing is a great way to get your company's website to appear at the top of the search engines right away, driving qualified traffic to your website.

Social Media Marketing

There is a lot of buzz around Social Media (Facebook, Twitter, Instagram, LinkedIn, YouTube), but how can it be utilized by a small business which is just starting out? How can you use social media to grow your business? Just look at the staggering statistics for Facebook:

- More than 500 million active users
- 50% of active users log-on to Facebook on any given day
- Average user has 130 connections
- People spend over 700 billion minutes per month on Facebook

So, how can you employ this amazing tool to grow your business? Use it to connect with your personal sphere of influence, past and new customers. By doing so, you can solidify and maintain existing relationships, remain top-of-mind, and ultimately increase repeat and referral business.

You should also keep in mind that some (or most!) future customers will check out your Facebook page. They will want to see how active it is and see if you have bad reviews on there, or even if they know someone who has recommended you. You should be consistently posting pictures of the projects you have completed, along with any testimonials you get.

Most customer will not tell you that they looked you up and it influenced their decision to go with you, but it absolutely does.

Video Marketing

Did you know YouTube is the second-most used search engine on the market? Would you guess it is even ahead of Bing and Yahoo? It's true!

Millions of people conduct YouTube searches on a daily basis. Most business owners are so focused on SEO they completely neglect the opportunities that video and YouTube provide.

By implementing a Video Marketing Strategy for your business, you can get additional placement in search results for your keywords, enhance the effectiveness of your SEO efforts and improve visitor conversion.

Don't think that you have to be a video pro to do it – it's as simple as taking your smartphone and recording a video with your camera. Letting future customers get to know you a bit by seeing you on video can go a long way towards building the trust that is needed to make the purchase.

Email Marketing

Similar to Social Media Marketing, email marketing is a great way to remain top-of-mind with your customers and increase repeat business and referrals. Compared to direct mail and newsletters, email marketing is by far the most cost-effective means to communicate with your customers.

As we will discuss in the Email Marketing chapter, we feel email marketing can be used to effectively draw your customers into your social media world.

Quick tip here – the best business (as you almost certainly already know) is from previous customers. One of the best things you can do is send a monthly – or even quarterly – newsletter to them. It will keep you on their radar when it's time for the next job. This is especially true for your commercial customers. But don't discount the residential customers – you never know *who* they know that might need your help.

Paid Lead Service Sites

There is an array of services that will sell you leads on a "pay-per-lead" basis or a flat monthly fee.

- HomeAdvisor.com
- Angi.com
- Networx.com
- Etc...

While these leads tend to go to a number of different companies and will be less qualified than other sources, these Pay-Per-Lead services can be a profitable online marketing channel if executed correctly.

That being said, I can count on one hand the number of Paving Marketers prospects and clients that I've talked to who have told me they love HomeAdvisor.

Now that you have an understanding of each of the Internet marketing channels available, in the following chapters we will discuss how you can leverage them to connect with new customers and grow your business.

Where to Start?

With such a large amount of Internet marketing channels, where should you start? To completely dominate your market, you should be pursuing each of these online marketing opportunities over time.

However, you must first begin with the foundation - your website, organic rankings and social media/email. You should start looking at the various paid marketing opportunities when your website is set up correctly, ranking on search engines for your most important keywords in the organic, non-paid listings and you are actively engaging in social media activity.

If you have the budget, you should start running Google Ads right away. Done properly, it allows you to target the services you want to sell more of and get profitable, exclusive leads. We have found that the next biggest and most impactful opportunity is getting ranked organically and in the maps. You may then leverage the additional profits in paid marketing to further augment your growth.

Next, let's look at the fundamentals of your overall marketing strategy before pressing forward into full implementation.

3

Start With The Fundamentals

Before we delve into Internet Marketing, SEO, and Social Media Marketing, I want to be sure we have built a strong marketing foundation.

After talking with owners and leaders at various paving companies across the United States, I have come to the realization the vast majority of you tend to skip straight past the basic fundamentals of your marketing strategy and dive headfirst into tactics (Pay-Per-Click adverting, SEO, Social Media, etc.).

So, what do I mean when I say "Fundamentals"? All marketing has 3 core components:

- Message (what)
- Market (who)
- Media (how)

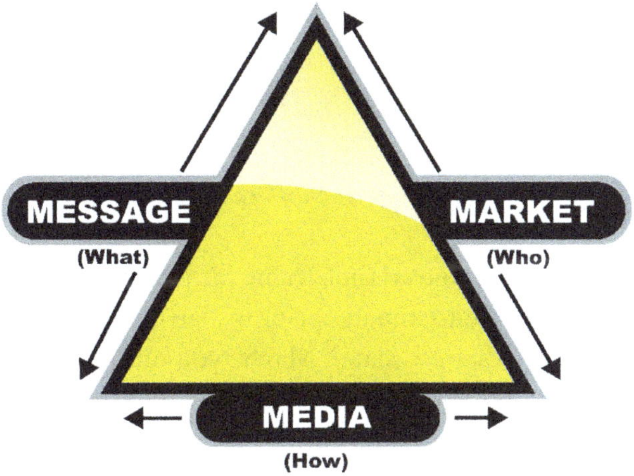

You have to have a unique "Message" (who you are, what you do, what makes you unique, and why someone should hire you rather than another business offering the same service), a specifically defined "Market" (who you sell to and who your best customers are), and then look at "Media" (where you can reach those best customers). The tactics (Pay-Per-Click, SEO, Social Media, Direct Mail, etc.) fall into the "Media" category.

If you focus solely on the Media or Tactics, you will likely fail regardless of how well-selected that Media is. With that being said, you need to scale back to the fundamentals. Invest the time and energy in fleshing out your "Message" and figuring out who your "Market" is. By doing so, ALL of your Media choices will be vastly more effective. How can you do that?

Spend a few minutes and THINK. Take out a scratch pad and

answer these questions:

Message

What do I do which is unique and different from my competitors?

Do you offer a guaranteed time frame for your appointments? Do you offer written estimates prior to starting work, promising to stand by that estimate? Maybe you offer a guarantee for all of your work and will look after any issues within a one-year period of time after the project is complete. Perhaps you offer a free consultation to showcase the services you have to offer to potential customers.

If you think about the psychology of a customer, what concerns or apprehensions do you think they have about hiring the services of a new business organization?

"They won't be able to finish the job on schedule, so I will probably have to waste a lot of time waiting around for them," or "They are going to be a crude mess and leave me with more work in the end," or "They are going to give me one price over the phone, tell me another when they start with the job and then charge me something VASTLY different once all is said and done."

How can you address your customers' common concerns in a unique way?

Answer these questions, and you will be able to define your

message.

> *Let me use Paving Marketers as an example – we are one of a very small number of marketing agencies that focus exclusively on paving companies, and we have a more comprehensive and thorough solution than anyone else. We have proven services tested over a decade and thousands of projects, and we're the only ones to back up our work with a $1,000,000 Guarantee. We're the #1 choice for paving companies.*

Market

Who is my ideal customer?

Please realize not everyone resides in your city nor within a 25-mile radius of your office. You need to be clear about the audience that you are looking to attract.

Look at your last 25 customers and evaluate who spent the most money, who had the highest profit margins, and who was genuinely pleased with your service. What are the unique characteristics of those good customers? Do they live in a particular area of town? Do they have a higher income level? How did they hear about your service offerings?

It could be that you want to focus on commercial work. You may subcontract out much of your paving work and want to focus on the more profitable (for you) sealcoating and asphalt maintenance jobs.

Start to define who your ideal customer is so you can put a marketing plan in place to attract similar customers.

This is also very important to keep in mind when crafting your message. You are talking to your future customers – make sure they know you are talking to them.

Most of our clients are looking for more commercial jobs. If that's you – think about the commercial clients you've had. What were they looking for when they hired someone and why did they choose you? Make sure potential customers can find that information.

> *At Paving Marketers, our market is paving companies. While the mix of services may be different, all would consider paving to be the core of their business. Some will do paving and concrete, some will do a lot of construction or sitework. Some will focus more on sealcoating and maintenance. Some only do pavers and hardscapes. But all consider themselves to be working in the paving industry. We work with sole proprietors who run the machines themselves, to small businesses with one or two crews, to more established companies with multiple locations and territories.*

Media

Where do I find my ideal customer online (and offline)?

Once you have fleshed out your Message and your Market, then you can start to think about Media. To determine what media will be most effective for you, you need to think about where you can reach your IDEAL customer.

Clearly, the Internet is a great "media" for connecting with your ideal customer who is proactively in the market for your services. Throughout the remainder of this book, we will be explaining the various Internet marketing channels and how you can use them to connect with your ideal customer.

Remember, you need to start with the FUNDAMENTALS (Message, Market and Media) before running headstrong into any marketing.

Don't forget about offline channels – postcards, newspapers, radio, TV, networking groups, etc. Take advantage of every channel available to you to get your Message out to your Market.

We're focused on the Internet here, but it all matters to grow your business.

Paving Marketers has a website that is the hub of our online operations, and we do SEO to help paving companies find us. We have a content strategy to consistently grow our internet presence for search terms.

We run Google Ads and Facebook Ads, and do monthly webinars and a podcast. We have a (free!) private Facebook Group to share tips and take questions from members.

We will participate in the National Pavement Expo and the World of Asphalt conferences, by hosting a booth and applying for speaking/training spots.

We send out lots of emails and also have salespeople calling out to potential customers.

4

How To Set Up Your Website

This chapter is all about how to setup your website. We are going to cover a lot of details as they relate to SEO, Google Maps Optimization, Pay-Per-Click Marketing, etc.

Without a properly designed and functioning website, those efforts will be put to waste. Before you can or even should begin exploring those options, you must have your website up and running.

Formats

Let's talk about website formats and the different options available to you when you are ready to start.

HTML Site – There are basic HTML pages and/or individual pages that can be incorporated into a website. This is how almost all websites were built several years ago. They had multiple pages hyper-linked together.

They are super-fast and secure, but unless you know how to code you'll need a web developer to build and update it. These tend to be the most expensive options.

Template Based Site Builders - Site builders, that you can obtain through providers such as Go Daddy, Website Tonight, and 1&1 are turnkey. You buy your domain and set up your website. I have found this type to be quite a bit less than ideal because you don't have a lot of flexibility. But, there are still a lot of sites in this format.

CMS Systems - Content Management Systems, like WordPress, Joomla, Drupal. There are many others but these are the big ones.

Given my experience with websites, a content management system (CMS) is ideal for a paving business. I say that because you have scalability. In any of these platforms, you have the ability to change your navigation on the fly, add as many pages as you need and easily scale out your site.

If you have your website built-in HTML format with graphics behind the website, and you wanted to add a new section, you would have to build that part from scratch.

You would have to go back to the graphics and modify all of the pages in order to add the new section to your navigational structure. With a CMS, everything is built behind code allowing the ability to apply easy edits and to add multiple pages.

As you will see in the search engine optimization section of the book, you will have the ability to have a page for each one of your services and each city in which you operate.

A CMS allows you to create your pages in a scalable format without having to mess around with the graphics or do anything that is difficult to control. Also, it is easy to access, modify, and update.

Using formats like WordPress and Joomla, you may access the back-end administrative area at something like yourcompany.com/login.

After entering your username and password, you will find there is a very easy to edit system with pages and posts which function similarly to Microsoft Word.

You can input text, import images and press “save”, forcing all new edits to be updated on your live website. It is easier than it looks and is very search engine friendly.

Content Management Systems have intelligently structured linking between pages and content, making it extremely search engine friendly. We have found this method tends to be better than regular HTML options.

In a lot of cases, a blog is going to be automatically bolted onto a CMS based website providing you with a section where you may feed updates. In the SEO chapter, we cover the importance of creating consistent updates and blogging regularly.

Another benefit of content management systems is being provided with a variety of plugins you can choose to incorporate on your website. You can easily pull in your social media feeds, YouTube Videos and check-ins.

You may also syndicate your website to automatically post any new updates to your social media profiles. You can add map integration where people can click to either get instructions or view a map to find out the areas which are served by your organization. There is a surplus of features available within a CMS that you can't necessarily do with a non-CMS type option.

Whether you are looking to build a website from the ground up, you are just getting started, or you feel like you simply need a redesign, I highly suggest that you do so in CMS, ideally in WordPress.

WordPress is a fantastic platform and very easy to use. It's the most adopted website platform available with many developers using it. It's constantly being updated and improved and I have found it to work very well for different businesses.

You have our stamp of approval to go out and build your website on a WordPress platform. It's what we use to build our client sites.

What Should Your Website Include?

So, what pages should your website have? What navigation structure should you create? Depending on your business, you will need to showcase different things. For most paving companies, though, the basics should be:

- Home
- About Us
- Our Services (you want one for each service you do)
- Our Service Area (You will understand what I mean once you read the SEO Chapter)
- Reviews and Testimonials
- Project Showcase
- Blog
- Contact Us

These are the core pages. Within "About Us," you might incorporate a drop- down menu for subcategories including "Meet the Team," "Why Choose Our Company," etc. I think that's very powerful. Potential customers want to get to know you a bit, they prefer that to a faceless, nameless, anonymous company.

You want to be able to drive people back to a "Why Choose Us" section, and, in some cases, if you are having issues recruiting and retaining good quality talent, you might want to have a "Careers" page under the "About Us" navigation, where a visitor can go and fill out an application and learn more about your organization.

Within "Our Services," you want to have the ability to list a drop-down listing the types of services that you offer. We discuss this to a great extent in the SEO chapter.

You want to have landing pages for each one of your services because they are going to be optimized with different keyword combinations.

Paving companies travel TO client locations, both residential and commercial, and a "Service Area" section will give you the ability to show a heat map of all of the locations that your team goes to, as well as a drop down menu that lists the sub-cities in which you operate within your market.

You can also build this out as an "areas served" section on the website. This is actually how we do it, for a number of reasons I won't get into here.

A "Reviews and Testimonials" page will provide a section to showcase what your customers are saying about you in text or video form.

You can also pull in reviews from sites such as Google Maps, Angi, and Yelp. Finally, of course, you will need a "Contact Us" page where web visitors have your general contact information.

These are the core things you should have on your website.

A Clear Description of Who You Are

A visitor who stumbles upon your website shouldn't have to do a thorough investigation to figure out who you are and what exactly you do.

This means it's important to clearly mention your business name and sum up your products or services above the fold section of your website. A clear and specific description will attract the visitor's attention immediately - within two to three seconds - and encourage them to spend time on your website.

Your Primary Contact Details

Outside of your navigational structure, what else should your website have? What other elements are going to help with conversion?

Well, you should always provide a primary phone number on every page of your website, in the upper right-hand corner. When somebody visits a page, their eyes are naturally drawn to the top section of the website where they can see the logo and the phone number.

People tend to expect that phone number will be somewhere in this location. It is ideal to have a prominent phone number, telling them to "call you now" for service in that section.

An Obvious Call to Action

Paving company websites should always make a web form available from which a customer can easily request an estimate.

Bear in mind that every visitor to your website is in a different situation and frame of mind. You may have someone that's on their phone or just leisurely looking to contact you to discuss a project and is able to simply pick up the phone and call you.

On the other hand, somebody who's in a work environment may not have the ability to stop what they are doing and make a phone call without drawing attention from his or her coworkers. However, they may be able to browse around online to find out what options are available.

Your potential customers may reach your website and be torn between making a call right at that moment, just scheduling the estimate, or wanting to have someone from your team contact them.

Make it easy for them to enter their information into a web form where they can provide their name, phone number, email address, and a note detailing their requests that they can send through online. It makes it easier and doesn't create any pressure.

Social Media Links

You also want to provide links to your social media profiles. Link to Facebook, Twitter and LinkedIn so customers can easily jump off, engage with you on social media, see what you're doing and be able to press that important "like," "follow" or "subscribe" button. It helps create a sense of authenticity when your customers get to see your social media content.

Customer Testimonials

Have a direct link which drives visitors to your online reviews and testimonials that we discussed previously.

You should also post your credentials either in the sidebar or in the header graphic, proving, for example, that you're BBB-accredited or a member of the local chamber of commerce or industry association.

This allows potential customers to rest assured that you are a credible organization, you're involved in the community and that you're less apt to provide them with poor service. They'll feel more comfortable doing business with you.

You definitely need to have your company name, address and phone number on every page of your website.

It is not critical that you list your address on each page because it will not be a determining factor in whether or not customers call you, but as I will explain in the Google Maps optimization chapter, having name, address and phone number consistency is critical for ranking on Google Maps.

It is a great strategy to have your name, address and phone number referenced on your website, ideally in the footer section. You need to have that contact information on all of your pages including the Contact Us page, of course.

Authentic Images

It's extremely important that you infuse personality into your website. By personality, I'm referring to authentic photos and videos.

Showcase your company, feature yourself, the business owner, and the people who work in the business: the office team, the crews, etc.

Showcase the office itself, the trucks and equipment if you have them. Don't use stock photography, but authentic imagery. This gives the visitor the chance to get to know, like and trust you, before they even pick up the phone. I've seen this tactic prove itself time and time again.

For example, let's say a general contractor visited two different paving company sites looking for a subcontractor. One of them is generic with the same stock images he's seen before. The other website shows the various equipment the paving company owns, including the exact machines he knows they will need to do the job. This authentic page converts 10 to 1. You must let your real personality and capability reflect on the website.

You must also craft messaging that explains why they should choose your company. Why should someone choose you over the competition?

Pull them down a path where they can start to learn more about why you are their best option. Where they can see your online reviews, and if they're kind of on the fence, where they can quickly locate some special offers and incentives that will drive action.

This will get them to contact you right away, as opposed to continuing to browse the web for someone else.

Mobile Website

The other major thing you want to think about, from the conversion perspective, is having a mobile-ready version of your website.

More and more people are accessing the Internet via smart phones such as iPhones and Android phones. Make sure the mobile version of your site isn't the same as your regular site.

It should be condensed, fitting their screen and giving them just the information that they need. It should integrate with their phone so all they have to do is press a button to call you.

People who are searching or accessing your website from a mobile device are in a different state of mind than the people that are browsing and finding you on a computer. Make it easy for them to get the information they need and to get in touch with you.

5

Why SEO Is So Important For Paving Companies

Most paving business owners already understand that the internet & search engines are *extremely* important to the long-term growth and sustainability of their company. But occasionally I am asked something like this:

"Why are search engines and search engine marketing so important to paving contractors?"

There are several good answers here – and it does need to be addressed. A huge number of paving contractors do not invest enough in their online marketing efforts and are hurting their business growth in the process.

Yellow Pages Are No Longer Effective

It used to be that the number one place consumers looked when they needed a paving contractor was the Yellow Pages. In today's market, very few people still reference the printed Yellow Pages. In fact, the newer generations have not even been exposed to the Yellow Pages and only know the internet to search for local businesses.

Where do they go now?

They look on the search engines (Google, Yahoo, Bing & others) and social media sites (Facebook & Twitter) asking for referrals from their friends and family.

- A recent survey of 2,000 consumers found that 86 percent of those surveyed used the internet to find a local business.
- 74 percent of the respondents said they use a search engine when they are looking for a local retail or service business.

If you are not showing up on page one of Google, Yahoo & Bing for the small business-related keywords in your area, then you are missing a major opportunity.

In the upcoming chapters we will show you how you can ensure that you put your best foot forward and show up in as many local paving contractor-related searches in your area as possible.

Understanding How Search Engines Work

Over the past ten years the way the search engines work has changed significantly - especially with the introduction of the Google Map listings to the search results for local search.

Most of the paving companies we talk with are confused about how the search engines work and the differences between the map listings, organic listings and the paid (pay-per-click) listings.

In this section we wanted to take a few minutes to DEMISTIFY the search engines and break down the anatomy of the search engine results page (SERPs). By understanding how each component works, you can formulate a strategy to maximize the results of each.

There are 3 core components of the search engines results page:

1. Paid / PPC Listings
2. Map Listings
3. Organic Listings

Let's take a look at them one by one.

Pay Per Click Listings

In the paid section of the search engines you are able to select the keywords that are relevant to you and then pay to be listed in this area. These are almost always at the top of the search results for "commercial-intent" keywords – i.e. the keywords searchers use when they want to buy something.

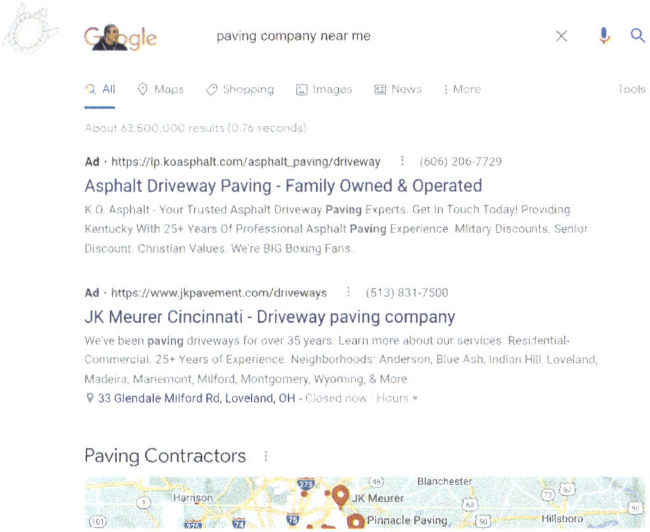

The reason these are called "Pay-Per-Click" or PPC is because rather than paying a flat monthly or daily fee for placement, you simply pay each time someone clicks on the link.

The cost per click is based on a bidding system. The company that bids the highest *with the best quality match between the ad, search, and landing page* gets the best placement. Great ads and landing pages can reduce your costs significantly – we have seen reductions of over 50%!

PPC is still a great way to market your business online, but it has to be approached carefully. PPC can get very expensive very fast, with some keywords costing as much as $60.00 per click or more in some industries.

Map Listings

The map listings have become very important because it is the first thing that comes up in the search results for most locally based searches after the ads. If someone searches "[your main keyword] + your city" chances are the map listings will be the first thing they look at.

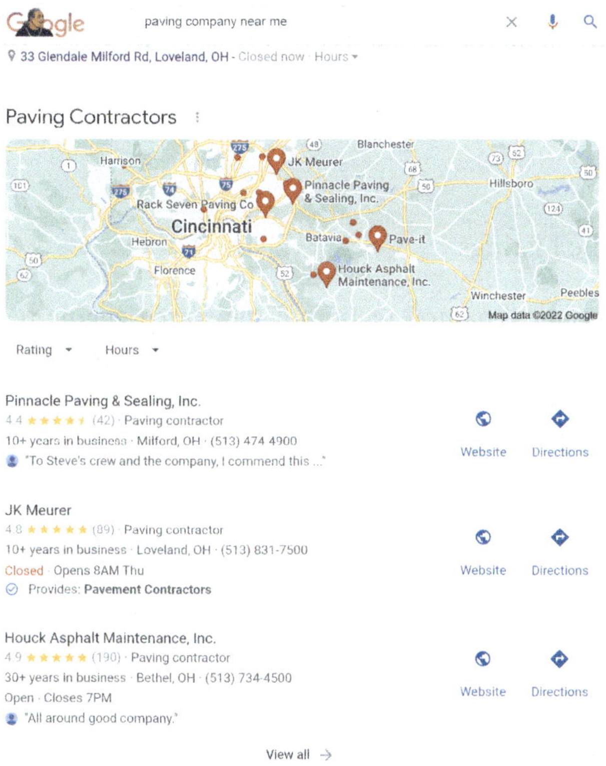

Unlike the paid section of the search engine, you can't buy your way into the map listings you have to earn it, and once you do, there is no per click cost associated with being in this section of the search engine.

Note that Google will sometimes show ads in the map listing, but typically on the "More Places" section. They experiment with placements quite a bit, and it changes from time to time as they do.

We will share our Google Maps optimization strategy with you later in this guide and show you exactly what needs to be done to obtain page one placement in the map section of the search results.

Organic Listings

The organic / natural section of the search engine results page appears directly beneath the map listings in many local searches, but appears directly beneath the paid listings in the absence of the map listings

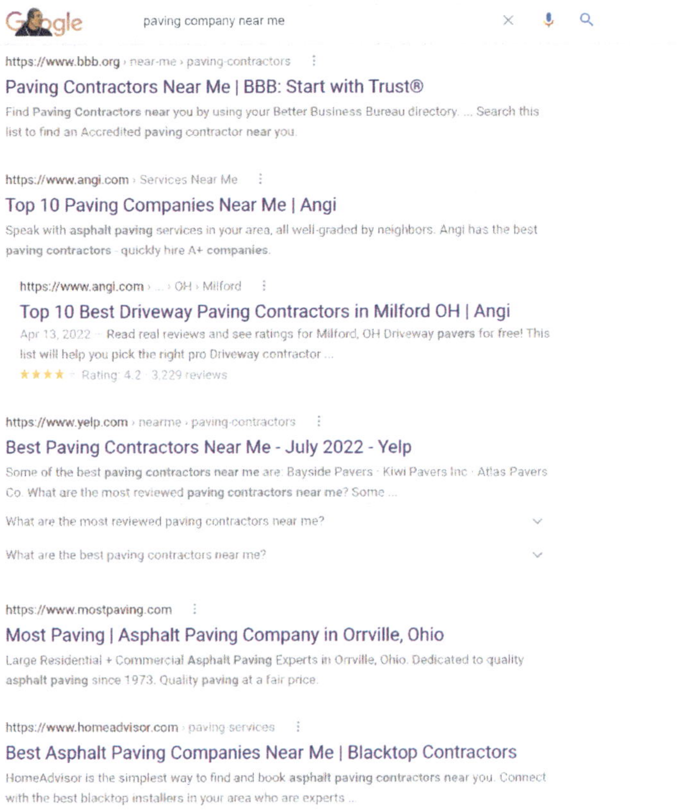

Similar to the map listings, you can't pay your way into this section of the search engines and there is no per click cost associated with it. We will share our search engine optimization strategy with you later in this guide.

Now that you understand the 3 major components of the search engine results and the differences between paid listings, map listings & organic listings you might wonder... "What section is most important?"

This is a question that we receive from paving business owners every day.

The answer is **all of them**.

All three components are important, and each should have a place in your online marketing program because you want to show up as often as possible when someone is searching for your services in your area. With that said, assuming you are operating on a limited budget and need to make each marketing dollar count; you need to focus your investment on the sections that are going to drive the strongest return on investment.

Research indicates that a vast majority of the population look directly at the organic & map listings when searching and their eyes simply glance over the paid listings.

However, many leads do come in through the paid listings – so active buyers tend not to ignore them. **Remember in the first chapter our data showed 1/3 of the leads came from Google Ads.**

If you are operating on a limited budget and need to get the best bang for your buck, you should start by focusing your efforts on the area that gets the most clicks at the lowest cost. We have found that placement in the organic and map section on the search engines can drive a better return on investment than PPC marketing – but it takes time to work, so if you need action right away, start with PPC.

So how can you get your paving company listed in the organic and map listings?

That is what we are going to be covering in the following chapters.

6

Getting Your Paving Company On Google Maps

For any local business, the best return-on-investment (ROI) lead generator is without question the Google Map listings. We are going to cover how to show up on the maps.

The Google Map result is what shows up when someone types in "your city" plus "your services" in Google.

Set Up Your Google Business Profile Listing

The most important thing you have to do is go to https://www.google.com/business/ and claim your "Google Business Profile" listing.

Before you do that, go ahead and check if your listing is already set up and just not claimed. Go to Google Maps (maps.google.com) and search for your business.

If your business has been around for a while, you are probably already in there. If it has not been claimed yet, you will see something like this:

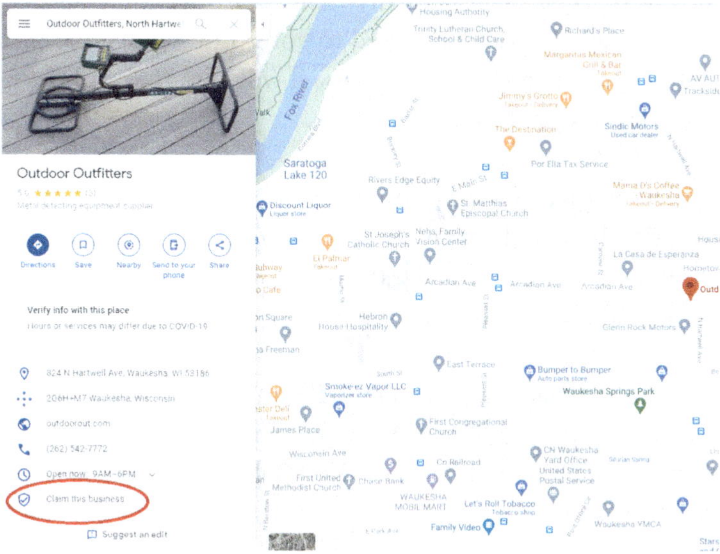

Go ahead and click "Claim this business" to start the process.

Some things to be aware of as you claim your Google Business Profile listing. The process is relatively simple. If you have a Gmail account or some type of Google account, Google should recognize that and let you use that to claim your listing. If you do not, you are going to need to go through the process of establishing a Google account so that you can claim your Google Business Profile listing.

Make sure you do not accidentally create a duplicate listing, especially if you already have one. It creates lots of problems and Google Customer Support is best described as worthless.

The most critical part of the setup process is to verify your business. They will typically mail a card to your business address with a code you need to enter into your GBP back end. Do not skip this step, because it will hurt your abilities to show up and rank well.

The actual setup is very straightforward - it is going to walk you step by step through the process. You are going to type in your company name, address, and phone number. Make sure all of that information is correct.

Use your actual company name. If your business is "Bob's All Seasons Paving," make sure that you enter, "Bob's All Seasons Paving," and not something else like "Bob's Paving" or "Bob's All Seasons, Your Dallas Paving Company." Do not add additional keywords in that name. It is against the Google Business Profile rules and policies and your listing could be deleted.

It is important that your Name, Address, and Phone Number (referred to as your "NAP") is correct. This is part of your online "fingerprint" and it will be critical that it is consistent as you take other steps in the ranking process.

If your address includes a Suite number, use it the same way each time. Either "Suite 300" or "#300" but not both in different places. Be consistent. If you are not sure which one to use, use the version Google shows when you search for your business.

Fill out all of the information fully and completely. Do not skip anything. If you do not have photos, go take them – both inside and outside of the office. Get a shot of your whole team together if you can.

Record a video introducing your business. It does not have to be "professionally done." Your customers are going to connect with real content – they are going to get a sense of who you are and what you are about. You only have 30 seconds to work with, so no need to overthink it!

List your hours, phone number, services, etc.

The most important section of all is your **categories**. This is how Google knows where to place your business in search results for Maps.

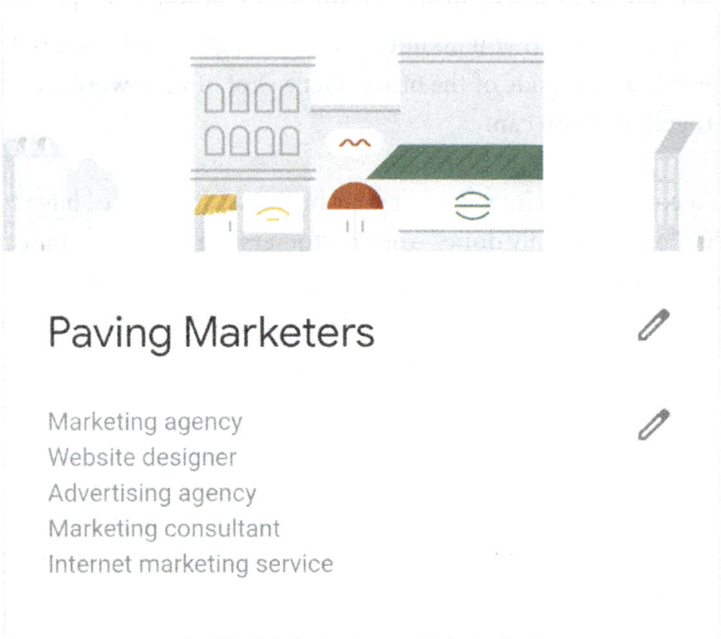

We are going to show you now how to pick them.

First, write down a list of your biggest competitors in your area. Pick the top 5 or 6 of them, especially those that you think have been doing a decent job online or have worked with SEO companies.

Now, go to Google Maps again and search for them – and write down the category you see.

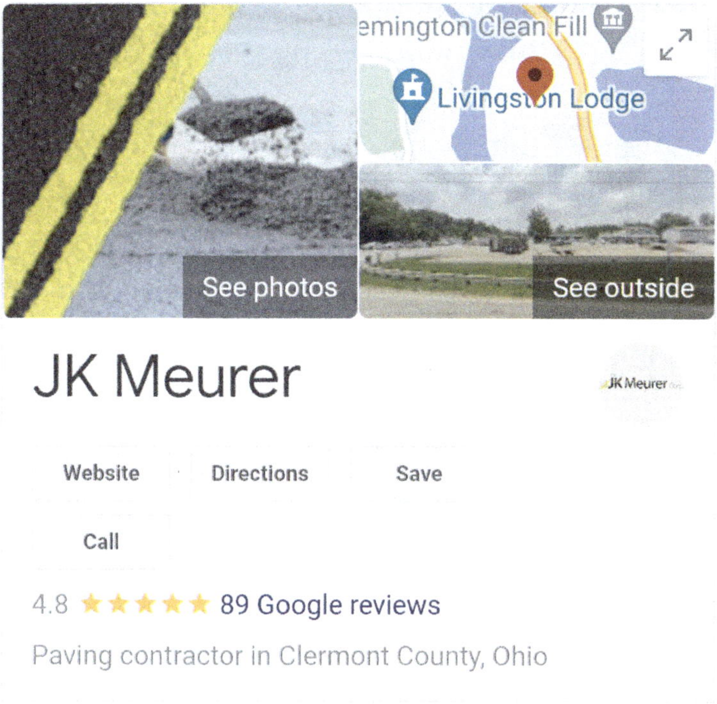
emington Clean Fill
Livingston Lodge
See photos
See outside
JK Meurer
JK Meurer
Website
Directions
Save
Call
4.8 89 Google reviews
Paving contractor in Clermont County, Ohio

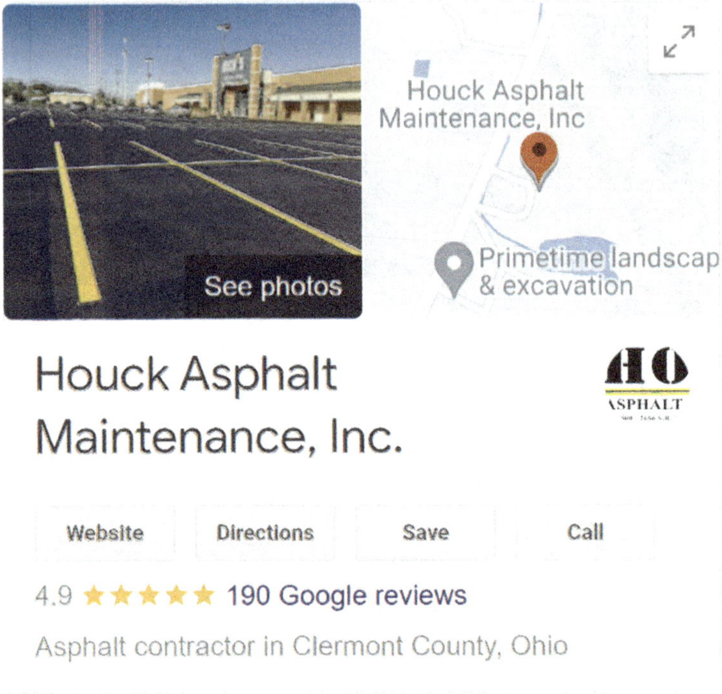
See photos
Houck Asphalt
Maintenance, Inc
Primetime landscap
& excavation
Houck Asphalt
Maintenance, Inc.
ASPHALT
Website
Directions
Save
Call
4.9 ★★★★★ 190 Google reviews
Asphalt contractor in Clermont County, Ohio

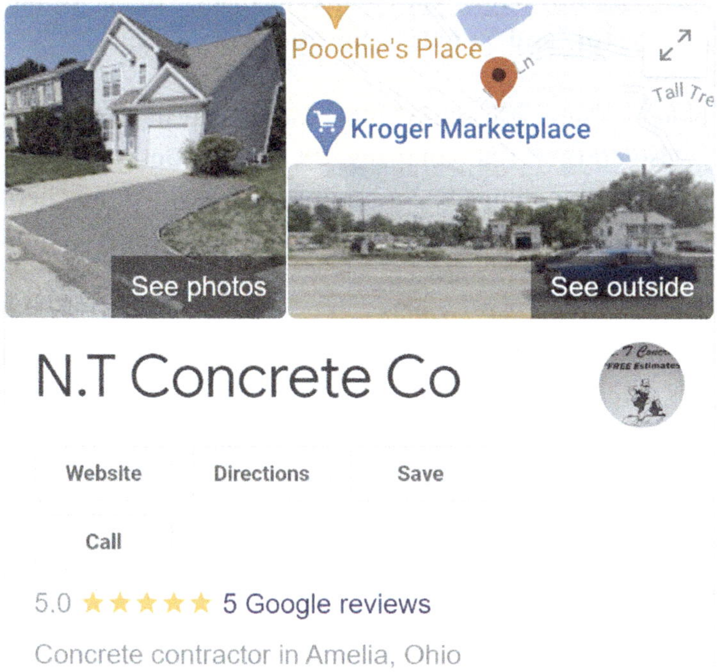

You might see 3-5 different terms in the categories, or you might see only one that shows up consistently. That is OK.

Now, search for those **categories** in Google Maps and see what shows up.

You should start seeing patterns. One category should show up more often than others when you see your competitors. *Choose that one as your primary category.*

For paving contractors: your primary category is

"paving contractor." Your sub-categories will be "asphalt contractor" and "concrete contractor."

Note – there are lots of other options available. There is also construction company, excavating contractor, road construction company, and more. But if you're a general paving company that does both asphalt and concrete work, this is the correct approach.

Then, add all of the other ones you saw as you were researching this as long as they are relevant to your business. You will end up with something like this:

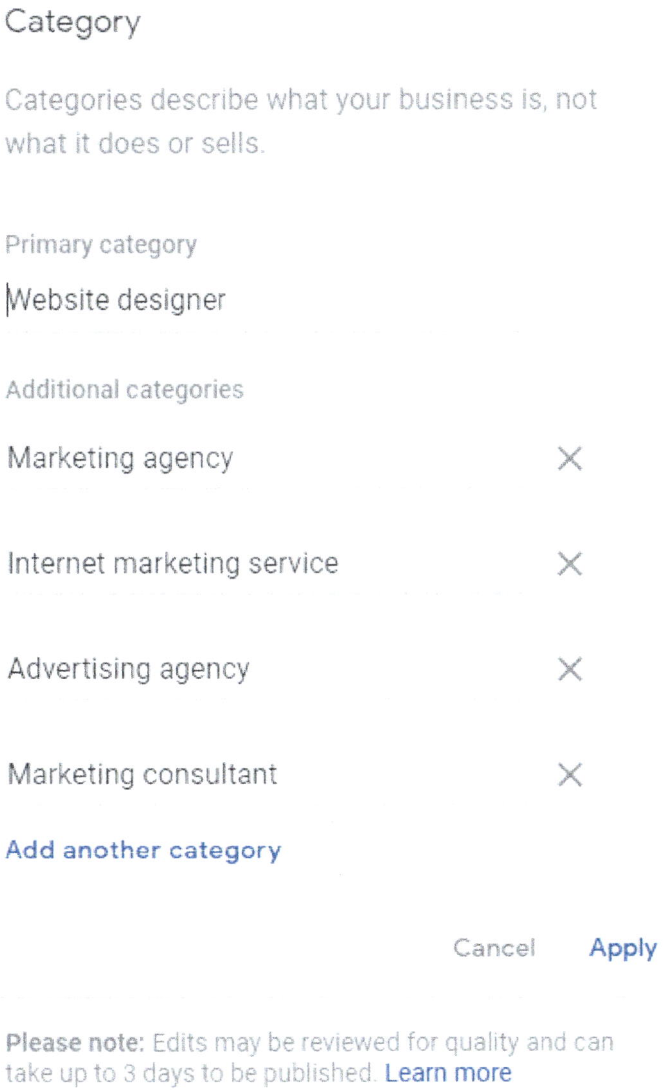
Category
Categories describe what your business is, not what it does or sells.
Primary category
Website designer
Additional categories
Marketing agency
Internet marketing service
Advertising agency
Marketing consultant
Add another category
Cancel
Apply
Please note: Edits may be reviewed for quality and can take up to 3 days to be published. Learn more

That is it, your GBP listing should be set up correctly!

Once you are verified, come back and test it from your office location. Type in your categories in Google Maps and see if you show up. If you know the keywords your customers would use to search for you, try those too. If you do not know them, we will cover that later.

Getting your listing in place is just the start of what you need to do. You are going to need to build a special kind of backlinks to support your listing, called *citations.*

I will use Paving Marketer's parent company Heaviside Group and one of our nearby competitors to illustrate how important this is – keeping identities private of course.

The reason for using Heaviside Group is that Paving Marketers does not try to rank in the local maps, because our market is the entire United States. Heaviside Group targets the Milwaukee-Waukesha, WI area, and the tri-state Cincinnati area, so local map results do matter.

When you just set up your Google Maps listing and leave it at that, you can expect to show up in a pattern that looks like this:

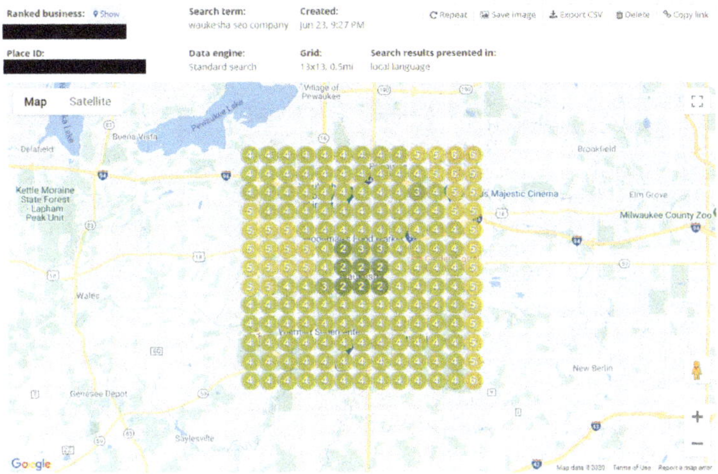

Each number is a spot on the grid where the maps ranking was measured – and is the location where the company showed up in the listings. Only spots 1, 2, and 3 are visible without clicking through to "more places" and those top spots get the vast majority of clicks.

You can see our competitor shows up for "Waukesha seo company" in the small area around their office but is essentially invisible to the rest of the city.

This is what you can expect to see when you first set up your GBP listing – but if you do the work of link building, you can expect to see something like this:

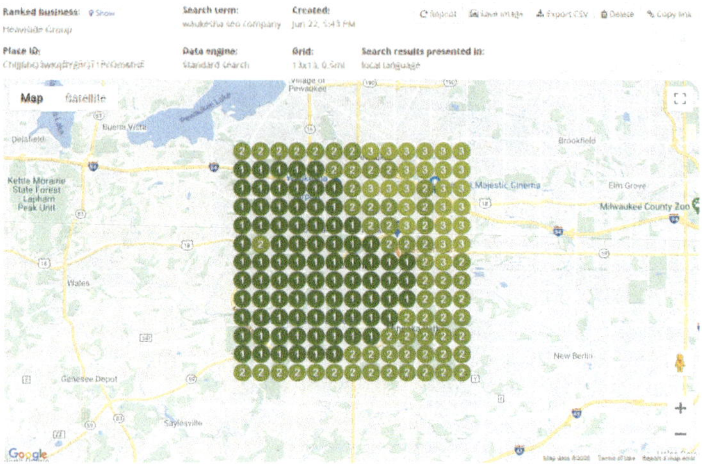

We are visible to everyone in the entire city. It also persists if someone does not use the "your city" + "your service" version:

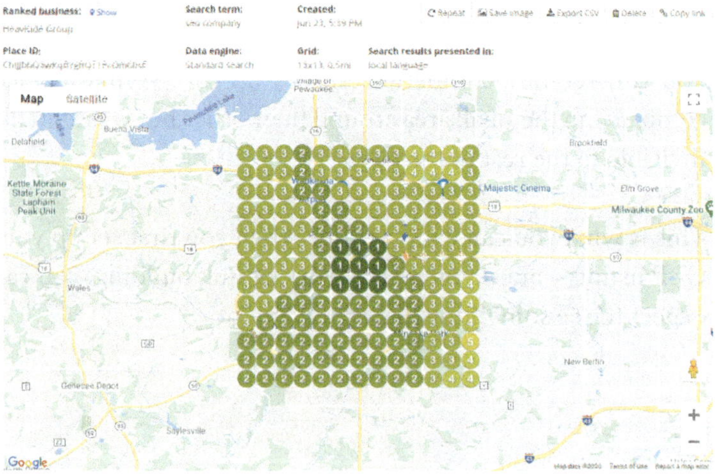

Keep in mind that Google gives a **strong** advantage to "close" businesses when someone is searching for a term. Most searches are mobile now, and when someone uses their phone Google knows exactly where they are and tends to show the closest businesses to them that match their query.

But – if your business sends **strong signals** that it is the authoritative or best one in the area, Google will show you over some nearer locations that might not be as strong.

There are more than 20 marketing companies in that area covered by the grid, or at least over 20 that actually show up in maps. *We are showing up in the top 3 map pack across the entire city.*

That is your goal with Google Maps. Part of that is driven by how you structure your site, but as I mentioned above building citations is a huge part of it.

Building Citations

If there is a site I *really* do not like, it is Yelp.

We have had the unfortunate situation of dealing with fake reviews at Heaviside Group – and one malcontent in particular went above and beyond, leaving the same fake review on every site he could find.

He was not even a customer of ours – we refused to work with him because his company dealt with adult-themed topics and drugs, and we did not want to participate in that. He took offense and left fake reviews everywhere.

It was a major pain, but I got them removed everywhere – except one place: you guessed it, Yelp.

This is the company that buried several actual reviews from customers and left up the one fake one – and refused to take it down after multiple complaints and calls. There are very few companies I will never work with, and Yelp tops the list.

I have talked to others who have had the same issue with them – they are a pain to deal with and frankly completely useless.

Except for one thing – a citation.

I tell this story because many local business owners can relate to Yelp problems – but also everyone knows who they are. It is a perfect example of a citation link.

Remember NAP? Name – Address – Phone. This is the core of citation building. Find as many sites as you can that will let you make a listing on there and do it. You are going to want dozens, if not hundreds of them.

Now – who has time for that? Not me. Fortunately, there are solutions for you to consider making the process easier.

We use BrightLocal – it locates relevant citations for our business and will go out and build them for us for a small fee.

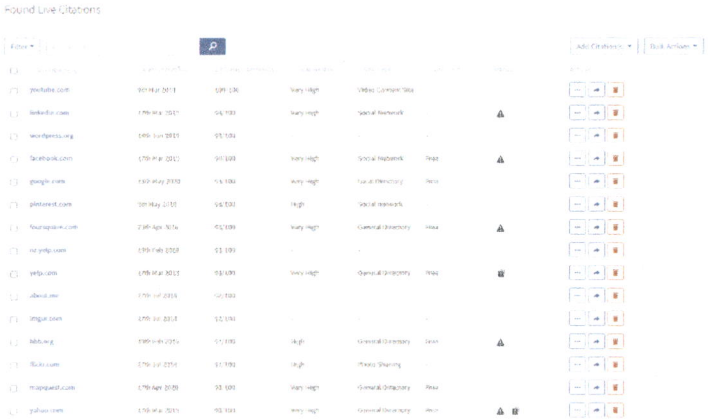

There are other options you can look at too. Moz Local offers a service, as does Yext. We also use Yext for our clients to give a huge boost.

They all do essentially the same thing – get your citations in order. The key thing here: your NAP must match your GBP listing and must match your website.

Pick one and get it done, that is it.

One more point to make here – you also want to build non-citation links to enhance the authority and strength of your domain. That has a very strong impact on the **organic** listing, but also influences your ability to show up in wider area on maps.

This is a pretty broad and complex topic to try to tackle here – there are lots of ways to go about doing this. We like to look at what links our competitors have and try to go get them – especially if those competitors are outranking us. There are lots of tools out there that can help you find out what links your competitors have – we use Ahrefs.

Here are a few examples – you might find that your competitors have a link from the local chamber of commerce. Are you a member of the chamber and have a link back to your site from them? If not, join. It is a good thing to do anyway.

You might see they have links from local newspapers. How did they get them? Can you get written up in an article on their website? Was it from a press release that was picked up?

They might have links from non-profit organizations in the area. Are they serving on the board? Did they make a contribution or gift, or volunteer their time?

Find out how your top competitors are getting links and do likewise.

Next, we are going to look at a factor that might surprise you.

Reviews

That negative review attack from that disgruntled "customer" was a real pain to deal with. It took a lot of time to resolve and it is still out there thanks to a certain terrible review site.

What do reviews have to do with ranking in the maps? Plenty!

There is no study that I am aware of that definitely shows ratings are a maps ranking factor – but there are certainly "secondary" metrics that indicate that they must be.

For example – one known ranking factor is the "click-through-rate" or CTR. This is what percent of the time searchers click on your result for that keyword. The better your CTR is relative to your ranking position, the more of a ranking boost you get. This is because Google's business model hinges on searchers getting the result they are looking for. If searchers tend to click on your site, that tells the algorithms that your site is clearly relevant to the search query.

Lots of positive ratings are a huge CTR-driver. Think about how you shop online. Are you clicking on the result that has only a few or poor reviews? Of course not – you are going to click on the one that has the most positive reviews.

We notice that the top-reviewed companies in an area tend to have a stronger maps presence. Whether that is from CTR or from reviews being included in the ranking algorithm is unclear, and it does not matter. Either way, you need to consistently get as many good reviews as you can.

There are a bunch of good options here too – we use custom software to help our clients reach out to their customers to get more reviews. BrightLocal has functionality that will work to do this. BirdEye is an option, as is NearbyNow. There are others too. Just pick one that makes sense to you and you will use and get it integrated into your customer service process.

Do not neglect this – it is one of the most important things you can do to take care of your online reputation.

Remember that goofball that gave us a bad review on Heaviside Group? We got rid of that one, but we have another fake one on Google we cannot shake. One-star, was never a customer, we have no idea who did it.

Can you tell?

No, you cannot, because we have 46 other 5-star reviews that bury it.

Most of your potential customers are not going to dig into the details right away – they will make snap judgements based on the overall rating. Anything below 4 and you are in trouble. They might investigate, but more than likely they are just going to click on your competitor who took reviews seriously.

The more reviews you have, the merrier. We have several marketing channels in place and have had a few difficult customers. We do not worry about those customers anymore, because no single unfair review can shake our online reputation – the quality of our work is very, very clear.

As Heaviside Group, we've done work on a number of platforms. Here's our total review results on one of them:

HEAVISIDE

heavisidegroup

Proven Digital Marketing Services

★★★★★ 4.8 (577 reviews)

If you take action on anything in this guide – take action on this. Bad reviews are the silent online leads killer.

Google Business Profile Optimization Best Practices

There are several best practices that you want to be aware of to properly optimize your Map listing.

- *Company Name* – As we mentioned above, always use your legal Company Name – do not stuff additional fields into the Name Field i.e. if your company name is "Joe's Paving" don't try to stuff additional keywords like "Joe's Paving – Dallas Paving Company". This would be against the Google Business Profile guidelines and will reduce your probability of ranking. It might work for a bit – but then you will get caught and slapped down. We have tested it – do not bother! It does work, but it's not worth the risk, as they do get banned.

- *Address* – On the "Address Field" use your EXACT legal address. Be intentional here. You want to ensure that you have the same address listed on your Google Business Profile listing as it is on all the other online directory listings like YellowPages.com, CitySearch.com, Yelp.com, etc. The consistency of your NAP (Name, Address, Phone Number) is very important for placement. Use either USPS format, or the format Google suggests.

- *Phone Number* – Use a local (not 800#) and use your real office number rather than a tracking number. We find that 800#'s don't rank well. If you use a tracking number it will not be consistent with your other citations and ultimately won't rank as well.

- *Categories* – You can use up to five categories, so use ALL five. Be sure to use categories that Google is telling you that your competitors are using and that reflect actual business you do. Don't put excavating contractor as a category if you don't do sitework.

- *Service Area & Location* – Make sure you set this up accurately. If you do not serve an area, do not say you do. If you have multiple locations, set separate Google Business Profiles for each one and make sure they do not overlap. Also, if you do not have a location in an area do not try to fake one with a UPS Mailbox or something like that. Google is wise to that one and it tends not to work.

- *Picture and Video* – Use this opportunity to upload authentic content about your company. Do not use stock photos, it is obvious and looks really bad. Just be authentic and give people an idea about who you are. Most people do not even look at this.

- *Reviews* – As we mentioned above, just make sure you have a process in place for this. Print out "Review Us" cards with instructions on how to do. Keep an eye out for very happy customers that might be willing to leave one for you. Send an email to your established client base with a link for them to click. There are lots of ways to do it!

7

Organic SEO Strategy For Paving Companies

SEO, or Search Engine Optimization, is the process of getting your website to show up in the organic (free / non-PPC) section of the search engines.

There are specific things that you can do both on and off your website to ensure that you show up when someone types "your service" + "your city" into Google, Yahoo or Bing. In all of our years working with small business clients in some of the most competitive markets in the United States, we have developed a proven strategy that consistently gets our clients to the top of the search engines and we are sharing it with you in this section.

Build Out Your Website To Capture More Search Terms

Search engines rank *pages*, not websites. Each page on your website can really only be successfully optimized for **one** main keyword.

A typical small business site has only 5-6 pages (Home – About Us – Our Services – Coupons – Contact Us). That does not create a lot of opportunities to rank for different terms. Now, most pages will rank for more than one term – but they will be closely related. If you offer several different services, you are not going to rank for all of them with one page.

Many paving businesses provide a wide variety of services. Some do more construction work than others, some do concrete. By *building* out the website and creating separate pages for each of these services (combined with city modifiers), you can get listed on the search engines for each of those different keyword combinations. Here is an example:

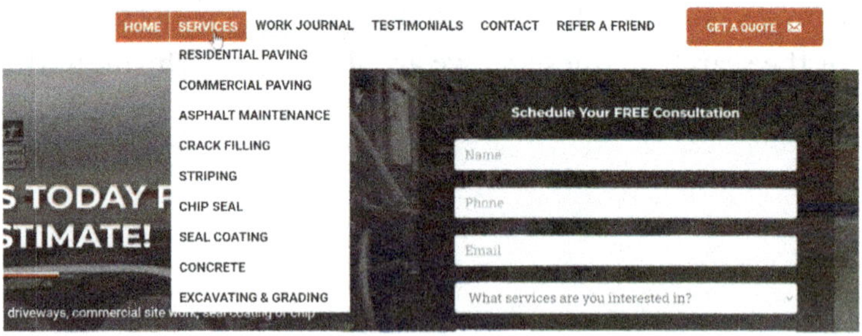

That shows how to build out the top menu. Then, in the footer, we have a small section that includes an Areas Served:

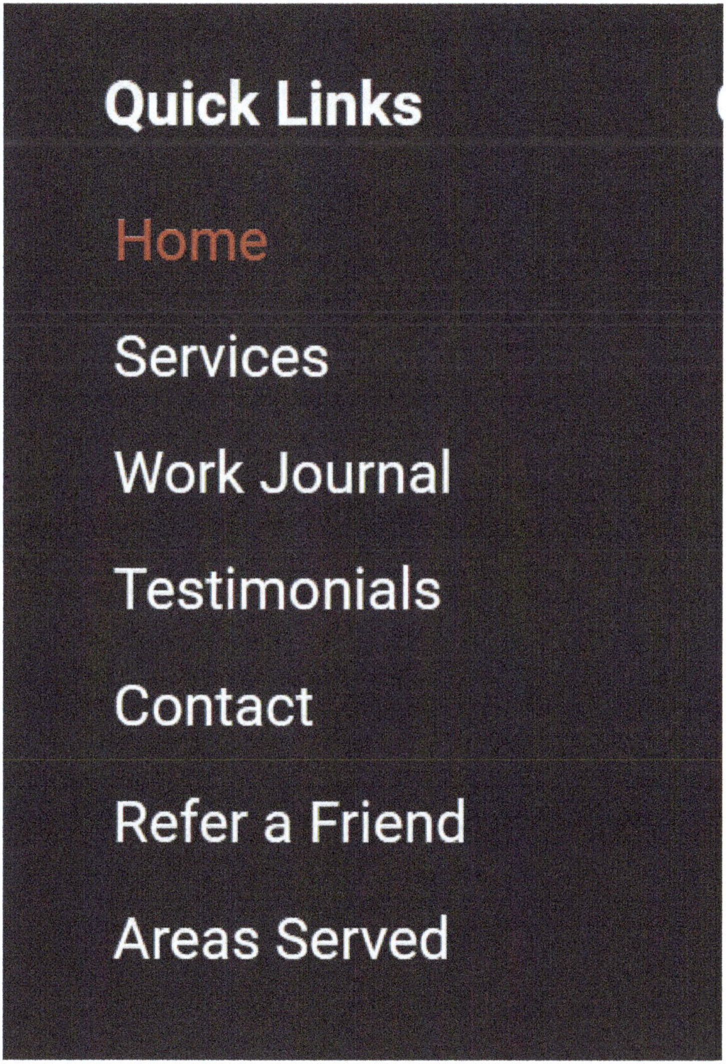

Part of that areas served looks like this:

So you see, each service they want to focus on is covered for each target city.

A quick note here about duplicate content. You cannot use exactly the same content for "Commercial Paving in San Antonio, TX" and "Commercial Paving in Canyon Lake, TX" or those pages will get penalized – Google's algorithms don't like that. The content on those pages has to be *unique*. Focus the page content more on the sub-area you are targeting and keep it simple. You do not need a long novel here; these sub-area keywords tend to be relatively less competitive and easier to rank for. Start with 500-750 words and see how it does for you.

Top Keywords For Paving Companies

The keywords you use on your website first depend on what services you offer, and as we've discussed, the cities you want to get jobs in. That being said, you also want to try to target keywords that have the highest search volume. Here's a list of the top ones in the US:

Optimize Pages for Search Engines

Once the pages are built for each of your core services and sub-pages, each of the pages need to be optimized from an SEO perspective so that the search engines understand what the page is about and list you for those words.

This is a very active area of development in SEO, and there is a huge move towards analyzing search engine results with statistical methods to see what ranking factors are the most important for each search term. We spend a lot of time doing this for our customers and it is become a key component of our on-page SEO strategy. That approach is very advanced and is outside of the scope of what most business owners will want to take on. Fortunately, there are some basics that are straightforward that can go a long way towards getting you ranked for the search terms that matter for your business.

If your website is built using WordPress, install the Yoast SEO plugin. There are others (we are partial to Rank Math) but Yoast is the most well known and is easy to use. This plugin will allow you to take care of most of these tasks without having to get into the website code.

Here are some of the most important items that need to be taken care of for on-page search engine optimization:

Unique Title Tag on each page – each page should have a unique title tag that no other page on your site has. It should include the keyword you want to rank that page for. We recommend this format: "Keyword Phrase You Want to Rank For | Your Brand" – for example, "Dallas Paving Company | Joe's Paving"

H1 Header Tag on each page – this should be the keyword phrase you want to rank for. So, from our example above we would use "Dallas Paving Company." Key point: do **not** use more than one H1 per page. Think of your web pages like an outline, and the H1 is the topic of our outline. The other header tags (H2, H3, and so on) are the bullet points beneath that topic. Would your outline make sense if it had more than one topic? No, and your page will not either. The H1 is the strongest signal in the body text area and you do not want to dilute it.

Other than that, just follow the guidelines that Yoast gives to optimize that page. They are not perfect, but it is going to get you close enough to be reasonably competitive. These will be things like adding keywords to the paragraph text and meta descriptions.

Make sure to create and set up the XML sitemap as well. Yoast will create one for you, and you will want to take that link and update Google Search Console with it. This is important because it lets Google know what pages you have on your website instead of relying on Google to find them. They are pretty good at doing that but giving them a sitemap ensures that all of your sub-pages will be found and likely indexed.

Inbound Links

Once your pages are built and the on-page optimization is complete, the next step is getting inbound links. The more competitive your niche and area are, the more of them you will likely need.

You have already built a solid link baseline with your citations, and we mentioned some competitor link-building possibilities previously. If you are not seeing enough traction with what you have done already you will have to get more aggressive in building links. They are still one of the strongest ranking signals that Google uses to assess website quality.

There are basically two approaches you can take here: do this yourself or hire a link-building service to do it for you.

We recommend the second approach. If you can allocate a budget of at least $300-$500 per month for links you can build some solid authority over time and enhance your competitiveness tremendously.

If you do not have a budget to do that, I would suggest continuing with the competitor backlink strategy. Those links can be challenging to get, and at some point you are going to run out of them, but they can be enough to do the job.

If you do have the budget, there are many different link providers out there. We have used https://authority.builders/ and https://nobs.link/ before.

That's it for on-page SEO – while each section has a ton more stuff you can do, and we do more for our clients, doing these things will put you ahead of many of your competitors and take you a long way towards winning the organic search results.

Content Marketing Strategies for Maintaining Relevance

Another highly important factor in SEO is maintaining relevance in your market by adding ongoing relevant updates to your website. In the Internet age, content is king.

Google Loves Fresh Content!

In some cases, with the changes in the algorithm, just because you've got a great website with the right title tags and all the best links, you may get discounted if they're not seeing fresh information posted on a consistent basis.

Google loves fresh content, and it is important to have a methodology where you are creating and posting content to your website on a regular basis. I want to give you a framework for figuring out what kind of content you could write, why you should create content, and how you can do it consistently.

First, you need to understand and accept that you need to

become a subject matter expert. You might not consider yourself a writer or a content creator, but you are a subject matter expert.

There are things you know that the general population does not. You're an expert when it comes to the service you are offering, and you have a team of people who are proficient in this area as well. You can create content on the topic that you know most about.

You can write about a variety of different topics including 1-2 relevant keywords with the same. You may not think it at first, but there are a lot of different topics in your industry you can come up with to create content about.

Types of Content

You should also consider that content doesn't have to be just written words. It's doesn't have to be just articles. Content can come in a variety of forms. The most popular are going to be articles, photos, videos and audio files. Stop and think about what content creation method works best for you.

Some people are great writers and that's their strength. Other people like to be on camera. I personally like to create videos. I'm very comfortable creating videos. Other people can talk (and they can talk your ear off about whatever topic they are passionate about!)

You can create content in many different ways. Because it is what I enjoy, I'll use video as an example. A business director can set up a camera and record himself explaining the services his company has to offer in the market, in the same manner that he would explain it to a customer.

Now you'll actually have multiple pieces of content. You'll have a video, which can be uploaded to YouTube, Vimeo, Meta Café, etc. This one piece of content can create multiple invaluable links to your website.

You can also take that video, save the audio portion of it, and you've got an audio clip. You can upload that audio file to your website and post on other various sites.

You can use a transcription service like Castingwords.com, for instance, where you upload the audio or video file and somebody converts it to text.

For a couple of bucks, you'll have a complete article comprised of what you said. Now you've got a piece of content you can post to your blog. You can put it on eHow or one of those other article directory sites.

Content Consistency

You want to create content on a consistent basis, using the blog on your website as the hub to post it, but then syndicating it to various sources.

Syndicating it to article directory sites if it's in text form, and sending it to video sites like Vimeo, Metacafe and YouTube.com if it's in video form. Doing this keeps the content fresh on your website/domain and creates a lot of authority, which is really going to help with the overall ranking of the website on the search engines.

You want to make sure you're appropriating each one of these link-building opportunities to maximize your rank-potential in your area. You might be surprised that the services you offer are highly competitive from a SEO perspective. There are a lot of companies who want to rank for the same keywords, and many of them have invested heavily in the Internet and in getting themselves higher in the search engines.

8

Website Conversion Fundamentals

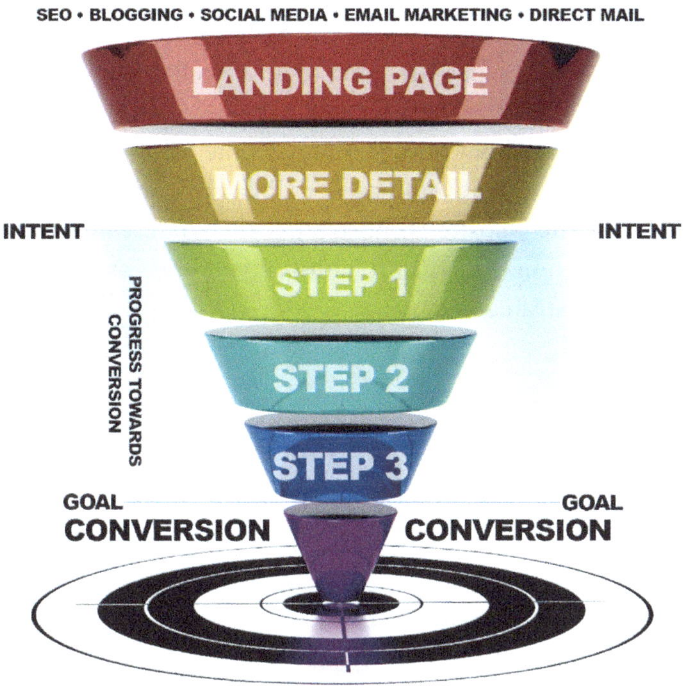

This chapter is all about website conversion fundamentals. We talk about how you need to set up your website, the messaging on your website and the navigational flow of your website to ensure maximum conversion and profitability from your entire online marketing effort.

The way I look at it is, you can have the best Pay Per Click campaign, search engine optimization, and be ranked number one on the Google Map. But, if the content and the structure of your website isn't set up in a way that's compelling for users, then it doesn't give them a reason to choose you over the competition, and it doesn't give them the information that they need to easily say, "You're the company that I am going to call for help." It's just not going to do as well as it could.

I want to talk about how we can take the traffic we're going to get from organic and Pay Per Click strategies, and make sure that the website is illustrating the correct message so we can maximize the profitability and revenue of our online marketing strategies.

Conversion Fundamentals

Be real. I talked about how people resonate with real people. They like to see the company, the people that they are going to be talking with on the phone and that are going to be going out to their home. So, as often as you can, avoid stock photography. Get a picture of the owner, the team, your office, or the front of the vehicle.

These things really draw people in and it gets them to feel that they would be working with real people because that is the kind of business that people want to deal with.

As for the content of your website, write messaging that draws them in and makes them connect. They're looking for an auto repair, dental clinic or interior painting company, so when they land on your home page, the first message they see should enforce the fact that they can trust you.

You should write something along the lines of, "Are you looking for a company that you can trust? Then you've come to the right place. We're operating on the same principles for the last 30 years: trust, innovation, and excellence."

Connect with them. Give them reasons to choose you and have a call to action, "Give us a call at this number for immediate service," or, "Click here to take advantage of our online specials and discounts." Remember, they've browsed around the Internet and have seen that there are hundreds of companies that they can choose from.

Give them some compelling information about who you are and why they would want to choose you. Ask them to call now for an appointment, and then draw them into a section where they can get an offer or a special discount. This is going to incentivize them to choose you and make that call right away.

What to Write

When it comes to the copy on the website, you want to address their specific concerns.

On your home page, you're going to want to show that you know what you're doing, have been in business for a long time (if you have), and that you can be trusted with an expensive and mission-critical project. You might say, "We've been paving Dallas for 50 years and have the reviews and references to back up our work. You can trust us with your project."

Pull them deeper into your website with "About Us" links,

special offers, and links to before and after images, especially for services pages. Those before and after pictures are a big deal.

Give them content that makes them think, "These guys know what they're doing," and draw them deeper and deeper into the website so they're more inclined to take the next step. Tell them why they should choose you over the competition. I talked about this in the "Message Market Media" chapter.

You should also, of course, have a web form on each of the pages of your website or, at a minimum, on the "Contact Us" page.

This is so that if they're not able or willing to pick up a phone, they can simply type in their name, email address, and phone number and let you contact them. Again, make sure that you've got your phone number on the top right-hand corner and that you've got a clear call to action telling them what to do next on every page of your website, under every block of text.

Keep in mind though, from our data, people call 4-5 times for every one form filled out. Your customers want to call you and talk about the project – make that as easy as possible for them to do.

Explain why they should choose you. Leverage personality. Be authentic. Integrate your photos into your website. It really, really helps with conversion.

Utilize your reviews, testimonials and videos. There's no

reason you can't create a simple video for each of the pages on your website, explaining what the service is, and why your business can do it best.

Some people are visual, they can see the content on the website and read it. Other people are more audible and would prefer to hear it.

If you can spend the time to provide both text and video, it really helps with conversion. Give them external proof. Take them out to the review sites where they can see testimonials on Angie's List, Google Maps, etc.

Show them what other people are saying, and you're going to significantly improve your conversion.

Example of a Paving Company Site that is Built to Convert

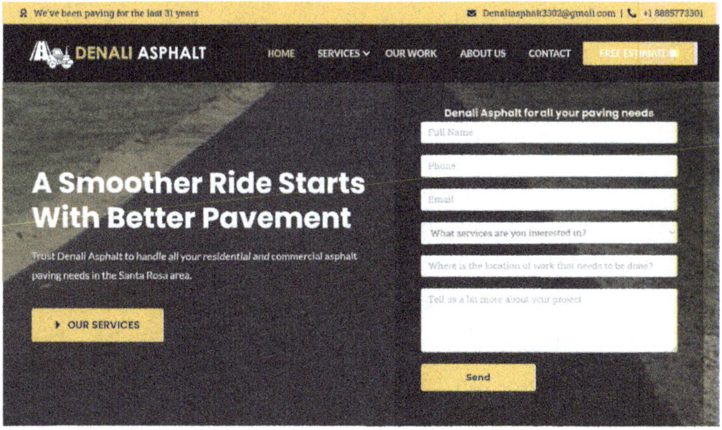

Internet marketing involves a lot of little things that are performed in sequence to get people to call your company when they are in need of your service. At the end of the month, it all comes down to the amount of calls you received and how much business was booked, right?

1. Company logo should always be in the top left hand side of the page. Their logo here is the perfect size. Sometimes clients tell me they want their logo to be triple this size. The reality is that few searchers know you from your company name, so occupying too much space with just your logo is a waste of valuable webpage real estate.
2. Your phone number is VERY IMPORTANT for the credibility of your company. It should be as close to the top right hand corner as possible. Make sure it's large and easy to find. Try not to make people search for it. It's frustrating for searchers and you have just a few seconds for them to find it before they may move on to another website. People always look to the top of the page for that vital piece of info.
3. Professionally shot photos. For a small investment, you could and should have a professional photographer come in and take some photos. You will use them everywhere. DIY photography is ok, but a professional photo is so much better. Drone footage of projects is even better.
4. A small blurb of text confirming the family-owned and operated company really brings it all together. People buy from people, not hidden companies. Personalize your website as much as possible. Your website is a marketing tool and its job is lead capture and to bring down as many

buying barriers as possible.

5. Main navigation. Your website's main navigation should be easy to find and the links should be clearly descriptive. Give people the option of moving around your website. One of Google's algorithms is how many pages a person visits and what their visit length was. Guide them down a path without confusing them. In other words, give them all the information they need in as few clicks as possible, but provide them the option of navigating around your site.
6. Some people want a way to contact you without calling. A contact form above the fold (the top half of the page) is great for capturing clients' info. It's also a great tool for building a contact list for email marketing down the road.
7. Get to the point right away without going into too much detail. The first paragraph of your text should give you a brief introduction of who you are and what you do. You can go into further detail on your About Us page.
8. Social media icons are a great tool because it allows potential visitors to see another side of your company. It's a great place to publish more videos and photos. Also, it's a great place to see how your company interacts with its community. From an SEO point of view, it helps build your company's social signal, something Google is paying more attention to. Social media is no longer just "marketing speak", it is a must when it comes to online marketing.
9. Don't forget about going mobile. The mobile web is huge and for the first time ever, mobile searching has passed desktop searching in the local market. It's only going to

continue to grow. The important thing with mobile is to make it easy and to get all of the important information front and center. Make sure everything is only a click away and always have your 'call us' button on top.

Website Conversion Factor Analysis

I have summarized the positive and negative points of the website that can affect the User-Friendly Interface of the website and the website conversions.

Homepage Banners

First, "Above the Fold" should be properly optimized. Above the fold areas are the sections of the webpage that are visible without the need for scrolling. This space is critical in regard to the user engagement and as such the most appealing attributes should be showcased in this section. Some of the most important conversion factors that should be present in the above the fold section is the following:

- Attention grabbing headlines
- Bullet points
- Calls to Action
- Form to capture leads

Please check the following Above the Fold banner for a reference:

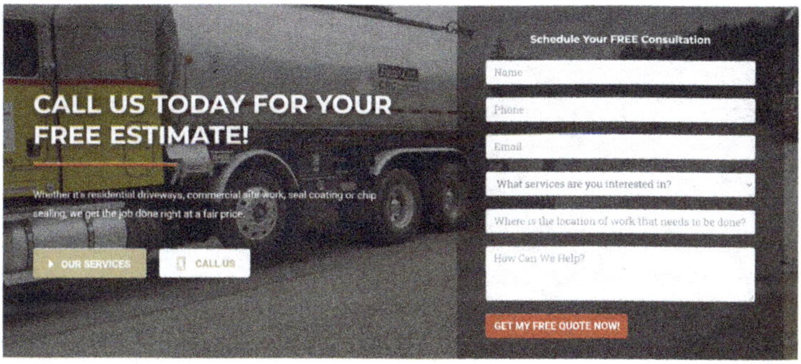

Second, you must include a proper section for "User Engagement" in the "above the fold" section of the website.

Ideally in the header section, there should be a downloadable whitepaper with an interesting title with a "Download Now" button and the user can download the same if they input their name and email address. Please check the following image for a reference:

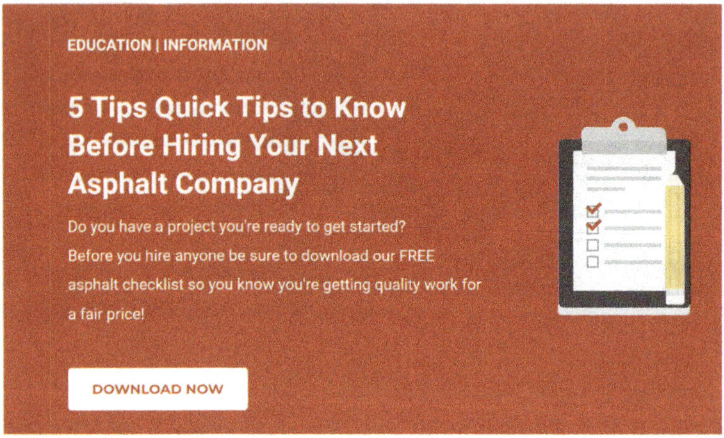

Company Profile

The home page needs to have a 60% company focus and 40% product focus.

Company credibility is the key to user engagement and any user needs to feel secure about the company before moving forward with browsing through the product section.

Therefore, it is important to have a brief company profile on your home page to let users know about "who you are", "why you are different" and "what your business is".

Ideally the home page should contain a brief overview about the company and a couple of bullets describing the salient features of the business. Please check the following example for a reference:

Latest News

There should be an enticing Latest News section on your Home Page in a professional press release format as Search engines give preference to sites that have press releases rather than articles on their home page.

The Press Release section should have at least two latest news, with a couple of lines about the news and a visible **Read More** button.

We deploy a "media room" on our client websites that feature press releases we do for them.

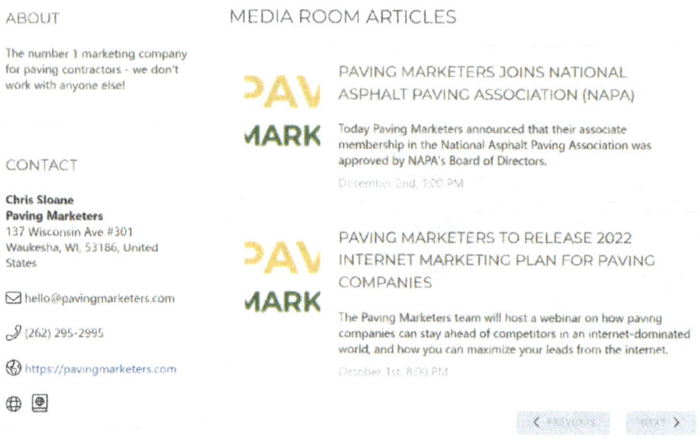

Blog

A blog is useful as it gives the visitors useful information and also gives credibility to the business as the visitor perceives that the business is up to date with the happenings in the industry.

Also, regarding the recent algorithm changes, updating the home page content at regular intervals is critically important in getting higher rankings in SERPs.

This is the reason the website should have a blog section in the home page similar to the following and the blogs should be updated regularly. Many customers use this to highlight recent projects:

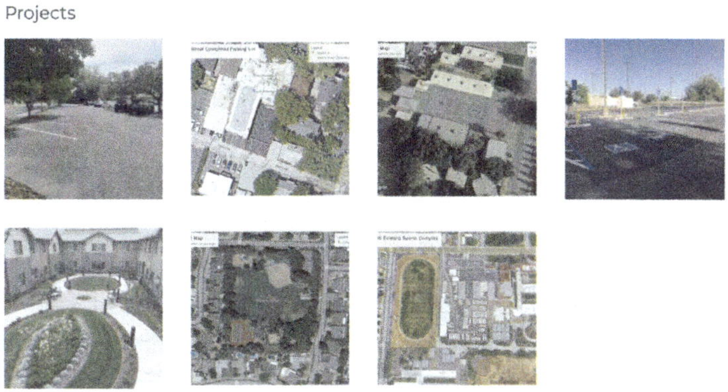

Testimonials

Testimonials are important since they earn credibility from your users.

The testimonials in your home page should have a "Read More" which will redirect to the testimonial page. They should also be clear and easy to read, for example:

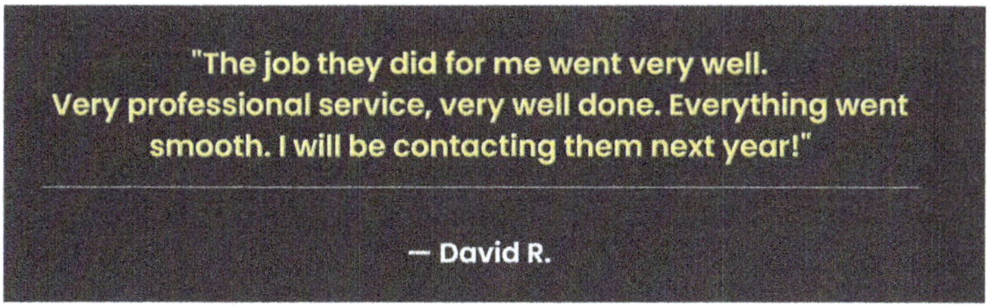

Optimize Your Website For Mobile Visitors

More and more of your customers are searching for service providers via mobile device. Here are just a few eye-opening mobile stats you should be aware of:

- Up to 70% of web traffic happens on a mobile device (CIODive, 2018)

- 80% of users used a mobile device to search the internet

in 2019 (Google)

- By 2020, the number of smartphone users is projected to reach 2.87 billion. (Google)

- World Advertising Research Center predicts that by 2025, three-quarters (¾) of users will access the Internet using a mobile device.

- More than one-quarter of all emails are opened on smartphones. (Source: Smart Insights, 2019)

- 40% of mobile users search for local businesses and often include the phrase "near me". (Source: Aumcore, 2019)

- It is predicted that mobile ad spend will reach almost 250 billion dollars by 2020. (Source: Statista)

- 61% of users will have a more positive opinion about your

business if you have a good responsive website. (Source: Smart Insights, 2019)

- 57% of users say they wouldn't recommend a company if their mobile website design is bad. (Google)

- By 2021, half of all eCommerce sales will be mobile sales. (Source: 99firms)

- According to BrizFeel, 49% of users use their mobile devices for shopping. (Google)

- 50% of B2B search queries today are made on smartphones and will grow to 70% by 2020 (Google)

- 96% of Facebook users access the app via a mobile device (Google, 2020)

Mobile smartphones can access websites, as well as perform a multitude of other tasks, which is why they have become more of a necessity than a luxury these days.

For you, as a paving business owner, this provides a unique opportunity to connect with local customers via their mobile devices.

Before you start to develop a mobile arsenal to drive more inbound calls, you must first figure out who your mobile competitors are. It is important to know who you are up against in mobile marketing so you can plan your strategies accordingly.

To effectively do this, you need to identify your closest competitors and learn what mobile techniques they are using to generate their sales.

Mobile-Optimized Websites

First, find out which of your competitors have a mobile-optimized website. One quick and easy way to find out is to pull up their website on your mobile phone.

Did it load quickly? Was it easy to find their contact information and other details that consumers tend to look for while on-the-go? Was it optimized to fit your phone screen? If so, they have invested in their business by making sure their mobile customers and prospects are taken care of.

Now, pull up your website on your mobile phone. If it's a nightmare, it's not your phone that is the problem, it's your website. This means you have been losing potential business.

Text Message Marketing

Next, figure out which of your competitors are using text message marketing. If your competitors are doing it, they are probably telling the world to "text 123 to example." If you see promotions such as this, they are using text messaging to build a list of repeat customers. We don't see this a lot with paving companies.

This is one of the most cost-effective and results-oriented forms of marketing today. Text message marketing allows your competition to draw in local consumers with a great offer. Then they send out occasional messages or coupon offers to keep them coming back to use their services.

Let's say one of your customers had plans to contact your business today after work, but they recently joined your closest competitors mobile list and had received a text coupon offer from them before they had the chance...

Who do you think the customer will call?

There are many other forms of mobile marketing your competitors could be using to capture the attention of local consumers such as mobile SEO, QR codes and mobile apps.

If they are using these methods, it may be in your best interest to start researching how your business can do it even better.

Analyze Your Current Mobile Marketing Status

What is your status when it comes to staying connected with local consumers using Mobile Marketing strategies?

Researching your competition is a necessary task if your goal is to become the local authority in your niche. But it is equally important for you to analyze where your business currently stands in order to move forward.

Are you currently running a mobile marketing campaign, but not seeing the results you want? Or, do you want to start a mobile marketing campaign but keep putting it off because you don't know where to begin?

Every business in your local area is in a crucial fight for more customers and profits. Therefore, in order to enjoy a spike in sales, your company can no longer ignore the profitability of ramping up your mobile efforts.

Analyze Your Mobile Status

Many business owners pump a lot of muscle in competing with similar businesses, while neglecting to take a close look at what they're doing.

Analyzing your mobile status will help you figure out which weaknesses are holding you back and which strong points can help you win the war.

You need to understand where your past efforts have taken you, as well as what your future has in store for you based on where you stand today.

For starters, it is crucial that you take note of what you are and aren't doing to generate more sales using mobile marketing.

Ask yourself the following:

- Is your mobile website user-friendly? Does it load within seconds or take forever to render properly? Does your mobile website have all the relevant information on it that consumers look for while on the go?

- Does your mobile website come up high in the rankings on mobile search engines, or is it nowhere to be found when local consumers perform a search for your "service + your city" on their mobile devices?

- Have you started to build a text marketing list? If so, what are you currently doing with that list? Are you focused on building a trusting relationship or are you spamming them with offers on a daily basis and getting high rates of opt-outs?

- Is your opt-in/call-to-action on all of your printed and web marketing materials?

- Are you using QR codes as an additional method of increasing awareness about your business? Do you have your QR codes on all your other marketing materials? Are you using them to direct traffic to your mobile website?

Do you currently use a mobile app to keep your audience engaged?

As you can see, there are a lot of things to consider when it comes to making sure your business is on the right track toward beating your local competition with mobile marketing.

Spy on Your Mobile Marketing Competitors

Do you want to know how your closest competitors are driving more business by using mobile marketing? Just take a look at their campaign yourself.

Mobile marketing has recently opened new doors for businesses that want to market their products and services by using mobile phones as personal "mini billboards". This has been enhanced by the fact that more and more people own mobile devices, and use them to find local products, services and businesses regularly.

To beat your competitors in the world of mobile marketing, you need to know what they are doing to be ahead of the curve. Digital technology is growing at astonishing rates and is not expected to slow down anytime soon.

This alone is causing many companies to be left behind when it comes to new-age technology.

Spying on your competitors' mobile marketing initiatives may seem like a daunting task, but it's not. In fact, all you need to do is identify which are taking most of your customers and let the research begin.

You should begin by visiting their mobile websites on your phone. Go through the websites and take note of the look and feel, the features and the traffic flow. Although your goal is NOT to copy exactly what they're doing, you could get a few pointers for your own mobile website.

Next, find out how their text message marketing campaigns operate simply by joining their mobile list. They probably have a text call-to-action placed everywhere, so opt-in and pay close attention to what happens throughout the entire process. This is the perfect way to get a first-hand look at their services, products, and promotions.

Are your competitors using QR codes to generate interest in their business? If so, whip out your mobile phone and scan their codes to see what lies behind them. Where do the QR codes take you? What type of incentives are they offering to get people to scan them?

Another thing you can investigate is your competitors' mobile applications. Download their apps and see what they're offering and how user-friendly they are.

The information you gain from your research should be used solely to set up your mobile marketing campaign that not only beats your competitors but also attracts new customers and keeps them loyal to your business.

Spying on your competitors is not illegal, but there are limits you should follow to remain fair. Under no circumstances should you use unethical measures to jeopardize your competition in your quest for mobile marketing.

Make Customers Call Your Business with Mobile Marketing

The secret to beating your competitors in any business is making your company more interesting to your target audience. There are several ways to do this using mobile marketing if you plan ahead, focus on the right things, and maintain your campaigns over time.

As much as you would like to boot your local competitors out of the picture, the fact is a lot of them will probably be using some of the same mobile marketing methods as you are.

So, your main focus should be geared toward making your customers choose your business over theirs. This is fairly easy to do if your efforts are consistent and persistent.

It is up to you which tools you use to work positively toward attracting new customers and keeping the ones you already have.

Here are a few tips which can work in your favor and help

local consumers choose you:

- You need to have a good website that is mobile-friendly and easily accessible by mobile phone users in your area. People are using their mobile phones to access the web to search for local products and services while on the go. Make sure your site loads quickly, gives them the exact information they need, and is easy to navigate.

- If you choose to start a text message marketing campaign, make sure your text messages offer great value, relay a clear message, and are short and informative. Also, be sure to send messages out consistently, yet conservatively. Create a careful balance that makes sense for your business and your target audience. Need a boost in getting new mobile subscribers? Give your customers and prospects a great incentive in exchange for opting-in and watch your list grow exponentially.

- Consumers love businesses who stay "on top" of the digital age. They expect you to have a website, be actively involved in their favorite social media outlets, and to be easily accessible from their mobile devices. Have a mobile app developed to aid in keeping your local consumers connected with your business. Implement the use of QR codes as a way to keep your local consumers engaged and provide them with "instant gratification."

- Mobile SEO should be used effectively to attract qualified traffic to your website. Mobile users search for local products and services constantly on their mobile devices when on the go. If your business does not rank in the results, there is major potential profit leak left for your competitors to scoop up.

Finding Your Business Basics

If somebody goes online, searches for your services, and gets to your website, they probably want to just get the basic information. They probably are not interested in learning a ton of information about you. They simply want to find who you are, where you're located, what your services are, and then press a button to book a service.

I have an example below of a mobile version of a site where they can just get the basic information, hit that "Book an Appointment" button, and then schedule an appointment. You should absolutely set up a mobile version of your site, give the basic information, and don't overcomplicate it.

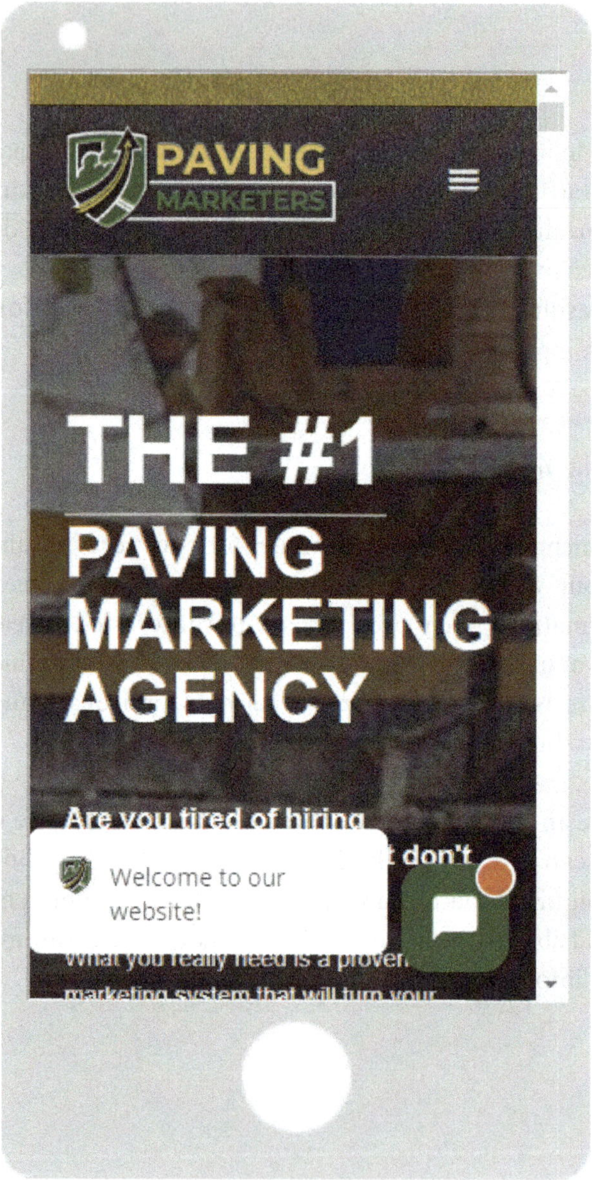
PAVING
MARKETERS
THE #1
PAVING
MARKETING
AGENCY
Are you tired of hiring
Welcome to our website!

Now that you have your website conversion fundamentals in order and have a proactive Mobile Marketing plan, you can start to think about Social Media Marketing.

9

Social Media Strategy For Paving Companies

There is a lot of interest around social media (Facebook, Twitter, etc), but how can it be leveraged by paving business owners? How can you actually use social media to grow your paving company?

Some businesses tend to be more active on social media than others, but there are some commonalities that you should take advantage of.

Social Media is not for everyone – if you don't use it or don't have much patience for it, read this brief intro. I'll go into more detail later.

Introduction

There are two main things to understand here. First, social media is a huge source of "word of mouth." If you think about it, where do most conversations happen now? Sure, you still see people in person and chat with them – but far and away most social interaction occurs on these platforms. Potential customers are going to check out your business on there. They might ask their friends for recommendations. They will read your recommendations. In a lot of ways managing this is like managing your reviews – seek out activity here.

Another aspect to consider here is recency – if your last social media post was 2 years ago people may wonder if you are still doing business. It might seem silly, but for heavy social media consumers activity on the site can signify activity in the "real world." You want to keep your social media profiles up to date and active for the same reason you update your website footer every year – it tells people you are still active. (You do that, right? If your footer says copyright 2016, put down this book and go change that right now!)

The second main thing to understand about social media is that it has become a huge source of entertainment.

The latest statistics indicate that the average social media user spends **2 hours and 23 minutes per day** browsing their feeds.

Compare this to the numbers from the Q1 2019 Nielsen Total Audience Report about hours spent watching TV per day. People aged 50+ spend about 6.5 hours per day. Those aged

35-49 spent roughly 3.75 hours per day. The 18-34 age group *spent just under 2 hours per day.*

People under 35 spend more time on social media than they do watching TV.

This trend is not likely to reverse – and so your business needs a strategy to be visible there.

Unfortunately, Facebook wised up to this years ago and the chances of your social media posts getting much widespread traction are slim-to-none. The Facebook newsfeed is pay-to-play, and so you must consider running Facebook Ads.

This is a huge topic and is too broad to cover here, but we can go over some basic principles that will be helpful.

First – we do **not** recommend that you try to run Facebook Ads yourself unless you take the time to learn how to do so. The interface is complicated and confusing, and there are many pitfalls that can lead you to set them up incorrectly. You also need the Facebook Pixel installed on your website or you cannot take advantage of the tracking and optimization features that are available. You also lose some of your best targeting options, like showing ads to people that are statistically similar to visitors to your website.

Second – you have to carefully consider *where* you are sending that traffic. Dumping Facebook Ads visitors onto your homepage is not going to do much for you.

Facebook Ads are interruption marketing – similar to TV commercials, except you can click on them and interact with them. That is the power of them, but also the danger. People are not looking for your product or service when they are on Facebook, they are looking for cat videos or updates from friends they have not talked to in years. If you catch their attention and they interact, you must make it easy for them to do what you want them to do, or they are going to go right back to cat videos.

Third – do not boost posts. It does not do anything useful for you.

Fourth – there is one type of campaign that every single business should do on Facebook, and if you are not, you are missing sales.

You need to set up retargeting campaigns based on visitors to your website, so that anyone who visits your website sees an ad from you on Facebook. Everyone knows about these ads (why is that vacuum cleaner following me around on the internet???) and some people are annoyed by them, but they have consistently been shown to improve conversion rates. Why?

Because people shop, and they often do not make a decision right away. They may have checked out your website, and a few of your competitors, and ultimately decided "I'll do this later."

If you're showing them ads across the internet between the

time they looked at your site and the time they decide to take action, and your competitors are not, who do you think is more likely to be remembered and have the best chance at the sale?

There's a lot more that can be done here, but if you have up-to-date social media channels, engage your customers with content, get their recommendations, and run ads to let them know about your business you are way ahead of most companies out there.

Going Into More Detail

There is a lot of BUZZ around Social Media (Facebook, Twitter, YouTube, LinkedIn), but how can it be leveraged by a service provider? How can you use social media to grow your business?

In this chapter we are going to cover social media marketing for your business. I hope that by now, you've learned a lot about how to position your company online, how to rank well on the organic listings on Google Maps, and how to rank well in the organic non-paid listings.

Now, we're going to talk about social media marketing, and how you can utilize social media tools like Facebook, Twitter, and LinkedIn to grow your business.

As I talk to paving business owners throughout the country about Internet marketing and social media, I tend to get a puzzled look. The question is, "How in the world does all of this social media stuff apply to my business? How can I possibly use Facebook in a way that would help me increase my revenues, boost my estimates, and get more repeat business?"

I'd like to try and bridge the gap on where the "lowest-hanging fruit" for social media is in your business by asking, "What's your number one source of business today?"

Just stop and think, where does most of your revenue come from? You'll quickly come to the conclusion that your number one source of revenue is repeated and referral business.

The lifeblood of many paving businesses is your existing customers returning for services over time, and your existing customers referring you to their network. If social media is harnessed correctly, it gives you the ability to take that repeat and referral business, inject it with steroids, and take it to a whole new level.

Let me explain why I feel that it's a great place for you to really connect with your customers and get more repeat and referral business. Just a couple of Facebook stats gleaned from Google:

- Facebook currently has 2.37 billion users
- The average user has 338 friends
- Users check in an average of 14 times per day

If you can get your real customers, current and past (your sphere of influence) to connect with you on social media, such as Facebook and/or Twitter, your business is exposed to their 388 friends as soon as they "like" and follow your page.

It's almost as if they'd sent an email, or they'd sent a text message out to all their friends saying, "I recently received a service from this service provider in our area. The next time you need their services, why don't you think about them?" It's extremely powerful to gain exposure to their sphere of influence.

Another major advantage is that they've given you permission to remain top-of-mind with them. The average user, like I said, checks in 14 times per day. They login to check out the updates on their Facebook wall and to see the updates of all the companies and people they have liked or are friends with. If you're posting updates to your social media profiles, the people who have liked your page are going to see that new content whenever they login.

They are going to see an update and your logo. They're going to see some special offer or promotion, and it's going to pique their interest. Next time they need your services, who do you think they're going to call?

People ask for recommendations all of the time. I'm not a huge Facebook user, but I check in maybe once a day. I'm a member of local groups – think people who live in the same area – and I've seen several people *asking for paving company recommendations* in those groups.

Top of Mind Awareness

There is a higher probability folks who have liked your page are going to use you again, and refer you to their friends, because they remember you and had a good experience with your service offering. They know who you are.

You've remained top-of-mind. If you look at major companies like Coca Cola, Pepsi, and Lay's, they spend billions of dollars a year on advertising and promotions, through TV, radio, and print.

What's the whole thought process behind that? They're developing their brand, so they can maintain what we call "TOMA," top-of-mind awareness. Leveraging social media inside your existing sphere of influence is a great way to tap into that top-of-mind awareness.

Where should you start? Where can you start using social media, with all of the different platforms out there? With so many different social media tools, what should you be using?

Earlier, we talked about having a blog and putting out consistent updates. Well, blogging ties very nicely to your social media strategy. These are the social media profiles you definitely want to have set up and ready to roll in your business.

- Facebook
- Twitter
- LinkedIn
- YouTube
- HomeAdvisor (not really social media, but do it)
- Angi (not really social media, but do it)

Finding Your Followers

Let's talk strategy before we get into the granular details. Talk about high level. How do you leverage social media and how do you gain that initial following?

Well, first, you want to utilize email to get initial engagement. Having an active social media profile with daily updates is not worth a hill of beans if you don't have likes or views.

Now, at the same time, if you have thousands of irrelevant people that have pressed like on your website or on your Facebook profile, it's not going to work to your advantage if they're not people in your service area. They're not the target market that we discussed in the marketing fundamentals.

You want to make sure that you have a strategy to get your real customers and your true service area engaged with you in social media. You should leverage email to engage your customers to get to your social media profiles. This takes a multiple step process.

The first thing you want to do is build that list or go into your customer relationship management system, if you have one, and export the name and email addresses of your customers. Include current customers, past customers, sphere of influence of your friends, your business partners, the people that you do business with, and put them into an email.

Queue up a nice little message which says, "Hey, we appreciate your business. We appreciate your relationship over the years. We're getting active in social media and would love to have you engage with us. Please go to Facebook.com and press the Like button." Make sure to give them a direct link to your Facebook page.

There are a couple of things you can do. You can offer them an incentive, something of value like a coupon or a discount. Or, if you feel like you've got an active customer base that knows who you are and likes you, just ask them to do it as a favor.

You'll be able to start building that following. Now, you don't want to stop there. You don't want to just send one email out that says, "We're on social media." You now want to build it as part of your business.

Just Ask!

In the Google Maps Optimization chapter, I talked about having an email go out after service, thanking the customer for their business and asking them to go ahead and write a review for you on one of the various online directory sites.

Well, there's no reason you couldn't send a subsequent email to that contact, maybe a day or two later, which says, "By the way, we're actively involved in social media and would love it if you would engage with us." Then give them a direct link to your social media profiles where they can press like, subscribe, and follow to start engaging with you on social media.

The key is that it needs to be an automated process where you're typing your customer's name and their email address. These emails go out to everybody that you serve without any hiccups, and without any potential for dropping the ball. If you don't do it consistently, you won't get a true following - and you won't get your real customers engaging with you on these social media platforms.

That's step one. Leverage email to build that initial engagement and following of your real customers. Remember, we want authentic customers, not just throwaway links and subscribers.

Once you've got that part squared away, you have got to think about what you are going to post. What information are you going to put up and how frequently? You should post to your social media profiles once a day. If that seems like too much for your business, post once a week at a very minimum.

What to Post (and Why)

These should be informative posts. It should not be a sales pitch. It should not be, "Here's 10-percent off your next service."

You can do that every now and then but more than 80% of the time it should just be social content: "Here's a picture of a driveway we paved", "Man we're getting killed on asphalt prices here", "Check out this sealcoating job Bob did.", etc.

Keep it informational, keep it relevant, keep it social, and then you must engage. Social media isn't a one-way dialogue. You shouldn't be going to your social media profiles and pushing out updates that don't have any engagement. You shouldn't just be posting. You should be trying to get people to reply to your post: "Hey, that was funny", or "That's a beautiful picture", or "Thanks for that great tip," all of which you can reply back to.

Then, listen to what your fans are saying. Once you've got a flow – you've got 50, 70, 100 or a couple of thousand people that have liked you – you are going to be able to hear what they are saying as well. They might post something that's totally irrelevant to you, like "Hey, tomorrow's Billy's birthday." There is no reason that your organization couldn't reach out and say, "Hey, wish Billy a happy birthday for us!", from your company. They will think, "Wow, this is a company that cares. This is a company that's real and authentic."

Engaging in social media is probably a lost art. Most people that use social media just post one-way messages, which is not the idea. It's a social platform, so there should be conversation. There should be dialogue.

Fill in the Business Bio

The next thing you want to do is to develop your brand and make sure that you enhance the bio section on each one of these profiles. Within Facebook, Twitter and LinkedIn, you will have the option to fill in an 'About Us' or bio section. Write some interesting information about your business there.

Take the information from the 'About Us' page on your website where you talk about where you were founded, why you started the business, the service that you offer, etc., and pop that into the bio section on your social media profiles.

You also have the ability to put an icon on each one of these social profiles, and you want to make sure that you're using an image that represents your business. It can either be a head shot of the owner or it can be a logo.

Below is an example of a few social media icon options that

go from good to bad to a big no-no!

Good
Company Logo, even better if you are a well known brand

Good
Mary Thompson
President
Mr. Rooter

Bad
Glad you like shaggy, and maybe it's your knick name. But it's not relevant to your business

Very Bad
Drinking a beer while giving the middle finger, unbelievably common, but a poor choice

If your personality represents your brand, then it might be a good idea to use a nice head shot so that people connect and resonate with you. People tend to buy from individuals more than they buy from businesses because a business is an anonymous entity, and a person is someone that they feel they can get to know, like and trust.

Don't be like our bad examples, "Shaggy" or the "drunk contractor." Don't put a picture of yourself in a T-shirt with a beard grown out. Be professional. Represent yourself as an important part of the business. Stick with the examples on the left – the logo and/or the professional head shot, as opposed to Shaggy or a weekend photo of you doing something crude and lascivious.

It's all about branding, so make sure that you're leveraging the header graphic and the image icon. If there is an option for you to customize the background, do it! You want to make sure that your elements marry up with the overall branding of your business.

Make sure everything on your social media profiles is consistent with your website. On your website, you've got a color scheme, a logo, and maybe you have printed brochures. Be sure to keep a consistent flow, look, feel, and color scheme on all your social media profiles, website, and offline materials.

Posting Plans and Pointers

Don't forget to have a plan for social media. How often are you going to post? What types of posts are you going to put out there? Who is going to be responsible for posting them? How are you going to engage your customers? Which social media profiles is your business going to be involved with?

Remember that earlier we talked about the fundamentals of your marketing plan (market, message and media). Be sure that you have a clear understanding of who your customer is and who your ideal customer is. Then make sure that you are crafting a message that will resonate with that particular customer. It's important to consider all of these things as part of your social media strategy.

Don't just dive in. A common mistake would be to just setup the profile and start posting with no thought process or plan behind it. Think about it. What pages are you going to be on? What message are you going to put out? What color scheme are you going to use? Set all of that up and then get very specific about your target. Is your client the commercial type? Is your client a residential type?

One solid method is to schedule your post types on specific days, such as:

Monday, Wednesday and Friday are the days that you are going to put up tips. For example, DIY tips are a great place to get started and you can dish out expert tips related to your service offerings, etc. You'll also make your customers realize that the stuff you do is NOT something they want to do themselves.

Tuesday and Thursday, you'll post photos, such as pictures of really interesting things relative to your business, pictures that showcase your work effectively, before-and-after pictures of a job well done. Pictures that are interactive are also good choices.

Saturday and Sunday, you post promos or entertaining content.

I am not saying this is the editorial calendar you must follow. This is only an example. However, the point is to make it easy for yourself so that you know what is going up and when. Your posting process can be streamlined, and it can also be automated.

Leveraging Posts

When we talked about the blog in the SEO chapter, we went over leveraging content. Because content is king, you have to be creating updated information on a consistent basis.

This content can go up in various places. As you post a new piece of content, it can go to your Facebook and Twitter pages automatically. It can go straight out to Pinterest if it has a photo included, and you can take your blog content and syndicate it to recreate great social media content.

Remember, content isn't necessarily just written text. You are an expert in your craft. You know things that the average consumer doesn't, such as what to do in the event of an emergency, why somebody would want to consider a specific service offering versus another, or why somebody would want to consider a new service offering you have recently started.

You can either sit down and write about it, you can take an audio recorder and record yourself talking about it, or if you're comfortable on video, you can break out the camera phone and shoot a video talking about an issue your ideal consumer may be facing.

How 1 Equals 5

Once you make a video, you can get a lot more bang for your buck. That one piece of content can serve multiple functions. The first function can be posting videos up on social media or on websites where you can upload interesting clips and videos like YouTube or Vimeo.

One video post can result in several forms of content.

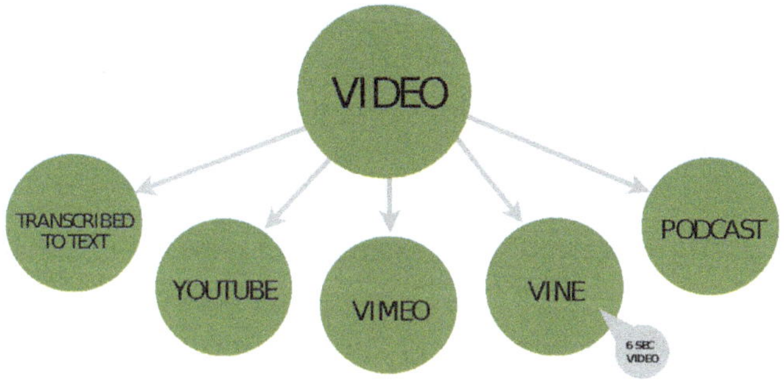

You can also have the video transcribed using a service like castingwords.com. There are various transcription services available.

That video of you talking about the benefits of your service offering can now be transcribed into text, which may then be used as a blog post and be syndicated into your social media profiles. Another step beyond that is using that same audio and turning it into an audio podcast you can have hosted on your website.

There are a lot of things you could do to take your content and work with the medium that you're most comfortable with. Some people like to write. Some people like to talk. Some people like to be on video. Figure out what you are most comfortable with and run with that. This is how you create social media content for your online marketing plan.

Remember, educational content that's published in multiple places gives you industry expert status. By publishing and getting picked up in industry listings, the local newspaper or a reputable blog, you are considered an expert. This is going to drive your credibility, which in turn, will result in more referrals.

I want to give you some examples of good social media posts.

Here's a good example of a "project finished" post:

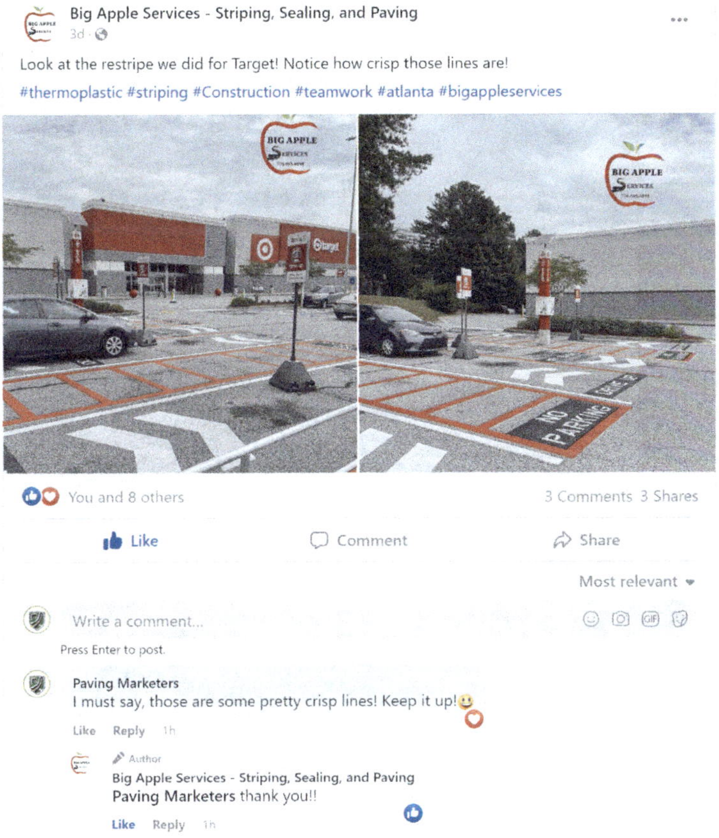

Here's an example of some good entertainment content from the Paving Nation Facebook Group:

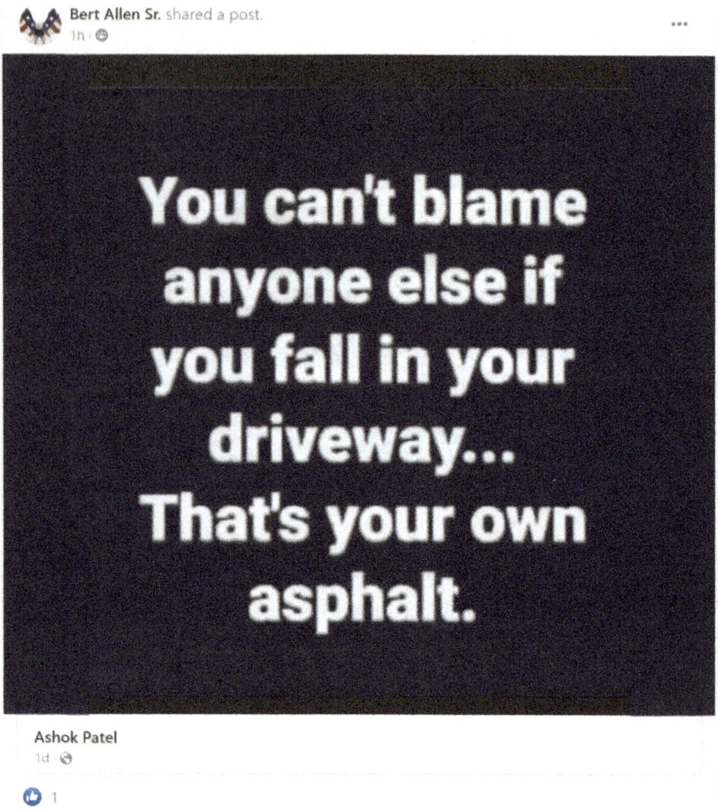

Here's one with some interesting content:

Rome Pritchett shared a post
11h · ...

Earthly Mission
3d ·
Core sample from the track at Indianapolis Speedway showing 108 years of paving history starting with brick.

That's pretty cool!

Do's and Don'ts of Posting:

1. Use the 80/20 rule for marketing messages. Put out 80% information and 20% marketing.

2. Keep it business related. Your political and religious beliefs are never a good mix with business.
3. Photos of your kids playing tee ball are good, but don't let it dominate your page.
4. Keep your vacation photos on your personal social sites.
5. Keep your business opinions, beliefs, and interests to yourself.

Sometimes knowing what not to post is more important than knowing what to post, because the natural tendency is to go to these social media profiles, and just post promotional material.

So, don't post a promo or deal every single time you log in. If you do that, everybody who liked or subscribed to your page will start to disappear before you know it. They'll stop subscribing, they'll unlike you, and they'll unfriend you.

You have to use the 80-20 rule for messaging: 80 percent informational and fun stuff, and only 20 percent should be promotional.

Keep it business related. You don't want to get into your political and religious beliefs, because if somebody disagrees with you, you can create a negative atmosphere. Don't tick off half of your potential customer base. Unless of course, you don't want to work with them. Then, knock yourself out.

In general, that's not something you want to do on your business profiles. You've got a personal profile for a reason. If you want to put your religious and political beliefs there, go for it. Just keep it off your business pages.

You may not necessarily want to put too many photos of your kids on your page, even if you're a personality brand. Don't let your kids and your family be the dominant positioning behind your business profile page.

Obviously, keep your vacation photos and again, your opinions and beliefs, off your business page. Family photos are another thing that should be kept primarily on your personal profile.

When and How to Engage

We talked about asking your customers to 'like you' on Facebook and asking your customers to write testimonials. We also talked about interaction and responding to your customer's actions. "Hey, thanks so much for the follow. We appreciate it." Or, if they write you a testimonial, make sure you blow that up.

Not only should you say thank you, but you should also share it. "Hey, Jean, thanks so much for the positive testimonial. We appreciate your feedback. We appreciate your business, and this is what keeps us going. This is what we're in this business for."

Then, you could take the testimonial and put it on your website or embed it on your website through the various widgets and short codes that Facebook provides.

For example, you create a post saying, "Seniors should live at a place where they can maintain their normal lifestyles and follow their interests. Let us know how we can help." Then, one of your followers says, "Wonderful caring staff. So lovingly devoted to those they serve." Then you respond: "Thank you for your comment! Our office phone number is 254-1799. We look forward to answering any questions you may have!" This is your engagement. You want people to make comments, and then you want to be able to talk back.

This is just a way to put out relevant content, and if you're paying attention to your feed, you can turn it into some great conversation. Again, you want to be active on social media.

It's a great way to get repeat or referral business. You need to be on Facebook, LinkedIn, Twitter and YouTube. You want to utilize email marketing to gain that initial following, and then post updates that are informative and not sales-oriented on a consistent basis and engage.

If you do this regularly and correctly, you're going to grow a nice following of real customers in your true service area. You're going to remain top-of-mind and it's going to help you grow your business in terms of the lifeblood of your organization, which is repeat and referral business.

Top Twitter Abbreviations You Should Know

Technical Twitter abbreviations:

- CC = Carbon-copy. Works the same way as email
- CX = Correction
- CT = Cuttweet. Another way of saying partial retweet

• DM = Direct message. A direct message is a message only you and the person who sent it can read

• HT = Hat tip. This is a way of attributing a link to another Twitter user

• MT = Modified tweet. This means the tweet you're looking at is a paraphrase of a tweet originally written by someone else

• PRT = Please retweet, a plea to put at the end of a tweet

• RT = Retweet. The tweet you're looking at was forwarded to you by another user

Industry Twitter Abbreviations:

- EM = Email Marketing
- EZine = Electronic Magazine
- FB = Facebook
- LI = LinkedIn
- SEO = Search Engine Optimization
- SM = Social Media
- SMM = Social Media Marketing
- SMO = Social Media Optimization
- SN = Social Network
- SROI = Social Return on Investment
- UGC = User Generated Content
- YT = YouTube

Common Hashtags and Chats:

- #BrandChat = private chat about branding
- #CMAD = Community Manager Appreciation Day
- #CMGR = Community Manger topic chat
- #FB = The user is sending this post to Facebook
- #FF = Short way of saying Follow Friday, or a recommen-

dation that others follow the user

- #in = the user is sending this post to LinkedIn
- #LI = This user is sending this post to LinkedIn
- #LinkedInChat = For general use questions and questions about marketing/self-promotion on LinkedIn
- #Mmchat = Marketing and social media chat
- #Pinchat = a chat for maximizing Pinterest use
- #SMManners = Social media manners chat
- #SMMeasure = For discussion of analytics and measurement
- #SMOchat = Social Media Optimization chat
- #SocialChat = Social media chat
- #SocialMedia = an all-inclusive chat for subjects big and small in the subject of Social Media

10

Video Marketing

Did you know that YouTube ranks second in search engines? Yes, it's actually ahead of Bing & Yahoo!

Most businesses are extremely focused on search engine optimization and/or PPC but neglect the opportunities that video and YouTube provide. Implementing a video marketing strategy for your business can get you additional placement in the search results for your targeted keywords, enhance the effectiveness of your SEO efforts and improve visitor conversion.

Why Use Video Marketing?

There are a number of reasons to use Video Marketing for your paving business.

First, it will increase your exposure on the search engines, giving you more placeholders for the keywords that are most important to you. Video marketing will enhance your SEO effort by driving visitors to your website and creating relevant links to your website, which will improve conversion.

Once somebody gets to your website, if there is good video on the home page and the subpages, it will resonate deeper with your potential customers than a site without video. This helps convert those visitors from just browsing around pages to actually picking up the phone and calling your office.

Again, YouTube is the second most used search engine there is. Obviously, Google is number one. One would think that Bing and Yahoo would be the other major search engines, but that just isn't the case.

There are significantly less videos than there are web pages on the Internet. So creating relevant and quality video content for YouTube and other video sharing sites is a really huge opportunity.

These videos will help you to connect with people and answer their questions when they're looking for information on what you do.

I talked about the fact that you can show up in search engines with an image next to it, and you can obtain multiple place holders on Google for the keywords that are most important to you. Here is a screenshot representing what this means:

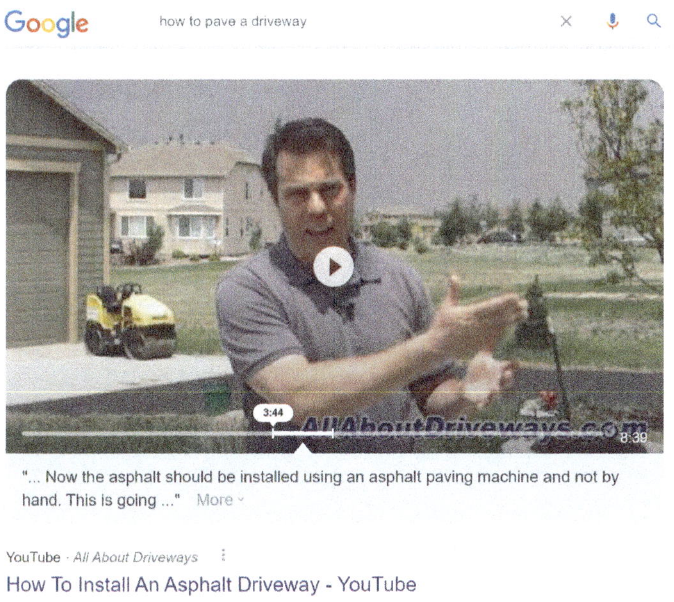

This website, allaboutdriveways.com, has great content about driveways. This particular blog explains the basics of paving a driveway. If we type in a search on Google for "How to pave a driveway," you'll see that his video shows up on page one with a few other listings. If you click that link, it takes you straight to a video.

If you do this right and you optimize your videos correctly (I'm going to show you exactly how in this chapter), you can start to have your video show up in the natural search on Google, which is extremely powerful. It also gives you the opportunity to have more placeholders for the various services that you provide.

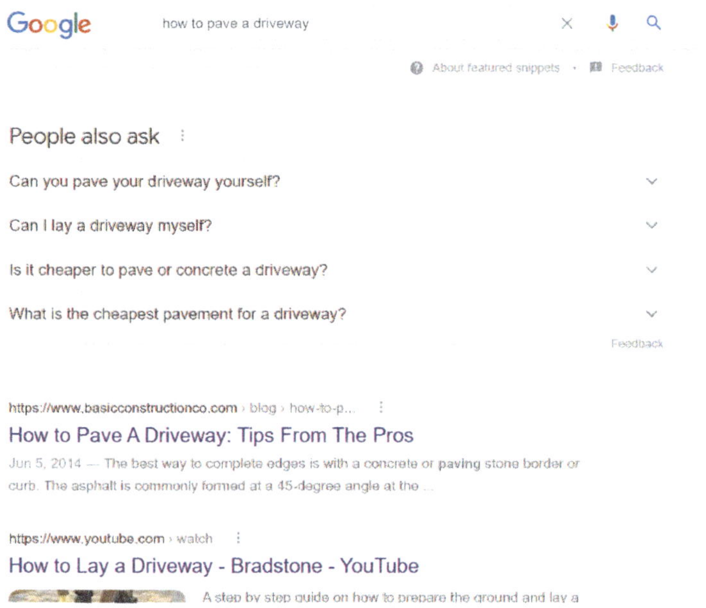

Below that video, you see a blog post from a different site after a questions snippet, and then several more videos. Videos have taken over a large amount of "how to" queries, and those are smart ones to target.

Whether your video ranks number one, number two, or number three, most of the time you'll notice that the video gets a much higher clickthrough rate.

This is because there is a large image displaying what that video is. Where are you going to click when you're searching? A static piece of text or the image? A lot of attention goes to those video results. This chapter explains how to incorporate these types of videos for your services and optimize them to show up just like this in your market.

Video Helps with Your Overall SEO Effort

The other thing that we can accomplish with video is the enhancement of our SEO efforts. As covered in the SEO chapter, links are critical for ranking. By creating good video content, you have the ability to drive inbound links to your website from high level video sites like YouTube and Vimeo.

Again, you don't want to have just the generic Home, About Us, Our Services, Contact Us pages on your website.

You want to have a page for each of your core services and products. Videos that link to those pages is going to help with that SEO effort. Also, you're going to find that video content on your website, and on the pages of your site, actually reduces your bounce rate and increases visitors' time on your site.

These are SEO factors. 'Bounce rate' refers to somebody getting to your page and clicking back immediately or browsing away. Google understands those actions as the page not being relevant to that search.

If the majority of the people that get to your site click off and leave right away, your bounce rate is high, and Google is going to start to show you less prominently in their results. That's part of the Google algorithm. The other factor is the amount of time spent on the site. If somebody gets to your page, stays there for ten seconds, and then moves on, the visit might not get treated like a bounce, but Google is still looking at the length on the site.

If you have a video and a visitor takes the time to watch it in its entirety, that's improving your website visit length statistics. Even if they only watch a couple seconds of the video, you have captured their attention long enough that Google is going to see your site is relevant.

Don't get confused by the notion that having video on your page automatically improves your SEO. That's not necessarily the case. But having people stay on your page longer and not bounce off does impact SEO. Here's an example of how you can drive some links with your videos.

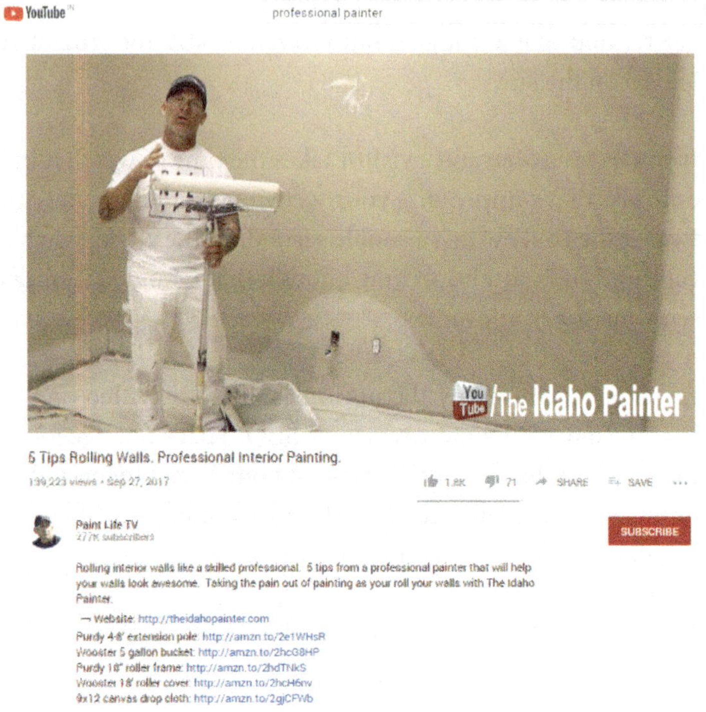

Here's an example of the YouTube channel on "Paint Live TV", which is a professional painting service in Idaho. You can see in the description area that they have included their website link: Idahopainter.com.

This link now connects you from YouTube to their site, and that's a relevant high impact link. You can do the same thing. I would suggest that you do not link to the home page, but rather to the specific subpage related to the video, like the interior painting tools or the surface preparation page.

Here's an example of a website TIM BROWN. We found his video in surfing for SEO services.

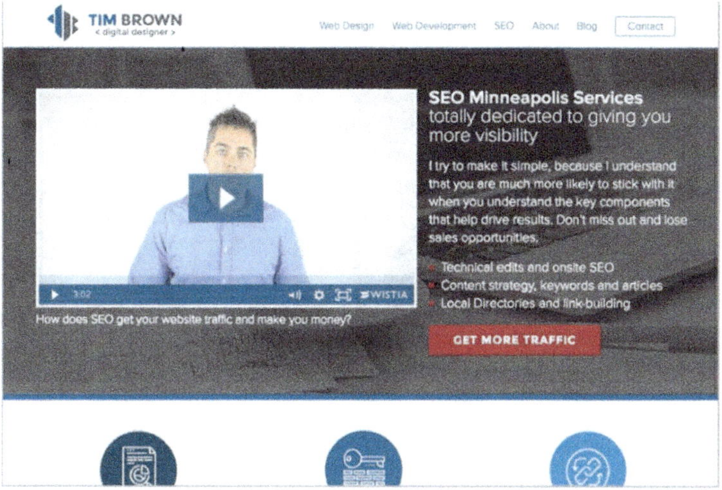

If you check the website, you will see a nice video above the fold section of the website. If you are interested in the service offering, you're most likely going to watch that video on the home page. Again, this is how you improve visitor time on your site and decrease the bounce rate.

People like to watch videos. It's very rare that you're going to see a video on subpages, but you'll find that if you do have that video content on the homepage banner or on your services page, people will take a couple minutes to watch it. Video is unexpected and it's more interesting than text. People enjoy watching someone explain the topic that they are researching.

Here's another example. I always recommend that your home page video be above the fold.

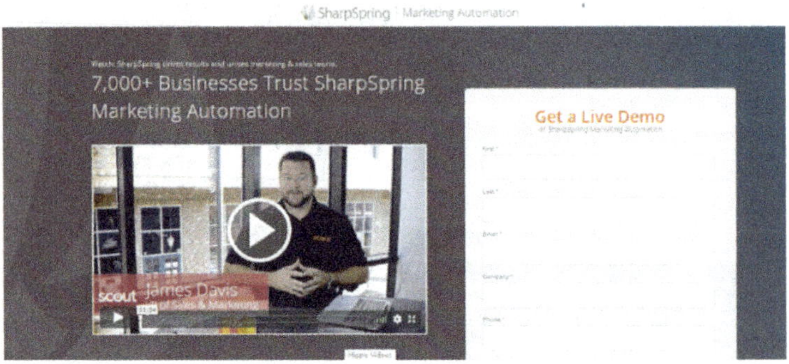

Above the Fold

Keeping a video above the fold means that you don't have to scroll down to see the most important information. Notice that as soon as this page is pulled up you immediately see the video.

You will want to do the same, providing an intro video about who you are and what you do. That video, placed correctly above the fold, will improve on-page site time and reduce your bounce rate.

I've mentioned the fact that video gives you more placement in search. It's going to give you better search engine optimization because you get the links from the video sites, you're improving your time on site, and reducing your bounce rate.

But the benefit of video that is probably even more powerful than anything, is that it's going to improve conversion.

You can have the best SEO strategy in the world and drive hundreds of people that are looking for your services to your home page or to your subpage daily. But, if it's not converting and people aren't picking up the phone and calling to hire you for your services after they visit your site, you're missing a major opportunity.

Improving Conversion with Video

Improving conversion is one of the main things having intelligent video on your site will do for you. The fact is that video clips resonate with people. They like video because it gives them the chance to get to know and trust you before they call you, especially if you follow my strategy rather than creating a super corporate video.

If you create authentic video of your team, the owner or your crew supervisor talking directly to the camera, connecting with you on an emotional level, answering questions and giving a strong call to action, your conversion rate will improve.

Video also gives you the ability to connect with different people. Everybody thinks in a different way. Some people are readers and will read all the content on a page. Some people are listeners, so if there's the opportunity to listen to something rather than read, they'll choose to listen.

Other people like something visual. Motion grabs their eye. By having video on your website, combined with text (I'm not saying to abandon text), you have the opportunity to connect with every type of person. Some people will watch the video and only connect with that, because they wouldn't take the time to read a plain text web page.

Here's a website of an online institute that offers private investigation training.

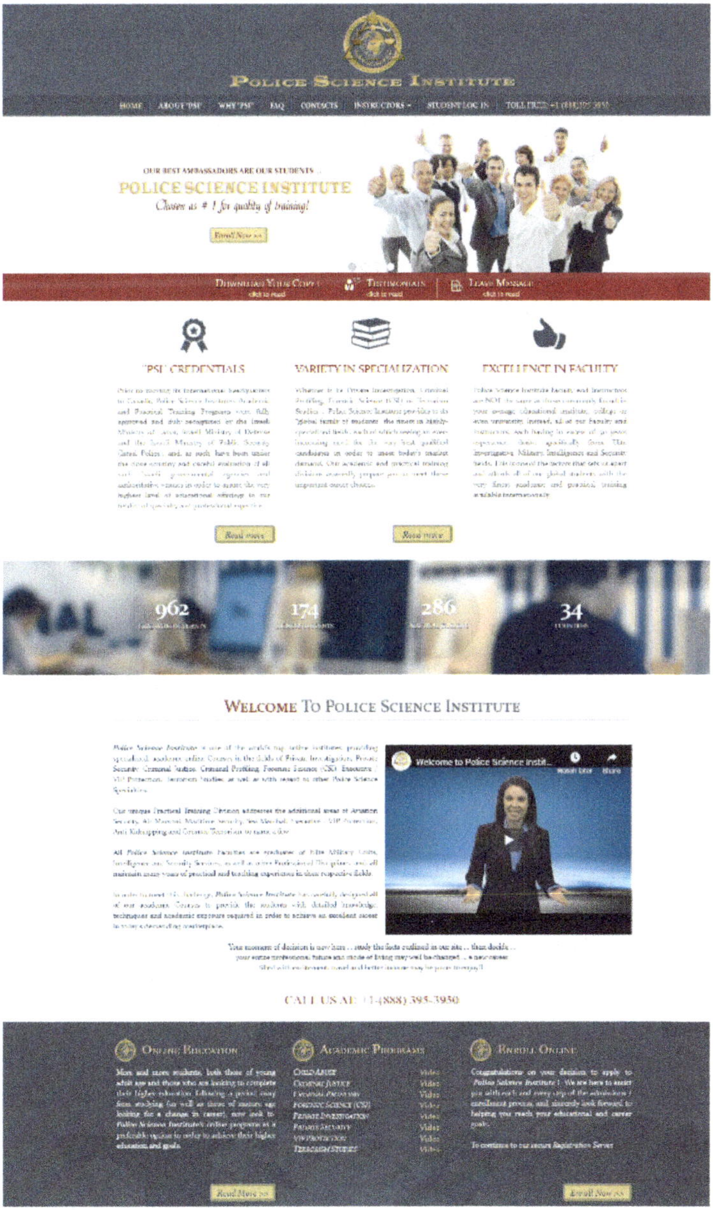
POLICE SCIENCE INSTITUTE
HOME
ABOUT 'PSI'
WHY 'PSI'
FAQ
CONTACTS
INSTRUCTORS
STUDENT LOG IN
OUR BEST AMBASSADORS ARE OUR STUDENTS ...
POLICE SCIENCE INSTITUTE
Chosen as # 1 for quality of training!
'PSI' CREDENTIALS
VARIETY IN SPECIALIZATION
EXCELLENCE IN FACULTY
Read more
Read more
962
174
286
34
WELCOME TO POLICE SCIENCE INSTITUTE
Welcome to Police Science Instit...
CALL US AT: +1-(888) 395-3950
Online Education
Academic Programs
Enroll Online

Upon visiting their website, you will see both the text and a video that explains what PSI has to offer. If you watch the video, and if the lady says something that's relevant to you that makes you feel connected, you may think, "Man, this is the right institute that I was looking for."

Do you think you would be more apt to call him over somebody who doesn't have that type of messaging on their website? Video on the site is going to improve conversion rates. It's going to make your phone ring more.

Leveraging Video

How can we leverage video? We understand that it's powerful, it's going to improve your SEO, it's going to help us get better placement on the search engines, and it could potentially help with conversion. How can we expand upon this?

What we want to do is create simple videos about your company, your services, and the most frequently asked questions. You are then going to upload those videos to YouTube and other video-sharing sites, and syndicate them to your website and social media profiles.

What type of video should you create? Like I keep saying, "People resonate with people." Keep it simple, be real and be personable. Put your real face on the camera, or the face of someone that represents your company. Be frank and to the point. It doesn't have to be a 20-minute video. An appropriate length would be 30 seconds to three minutes long, enough to get the message across.

Don't Overthink It!

Don't feel like you have to go all out and hire a high-end production crew or go out and buy an HD camera in order to make this happen. The reality is, you can create video clips using technology that you already have. If you've got a 4g smartphone or a webcam, you have the ability to create video content that will work for your website.

You don't need high-end editing software either. YouTube gives you the ability to upload regular video and edit it right within the system. By edit, I mean cropping and tailoring the video to begin and end where you wish. You can put your phone number down in the bottom area of the video as well as a link to your website. Or you can use a simple editing software like iMovie (free with Macintosh computers) and Movie Maker (free with the PC).

Using the technology that you already have, stand in front of a company sign with your logo or in your office, and talk to the camera; talk with the people that are visiting your website, because that's going to stick with them.

What Kind of Videos Should You Create?

You can create just about anything you want. But the ones that are going to be most relevant are the ones that pertain to your services.

The first video that I recommend you make is an introduction for your website. This can be as simple as, "Thank you so much for visiting the Joe's Paving Company website. We specialize in providing paving services to the Dallas area. These are the things that make us unique and why people tend to choose us. We'd love the opportunity to serve you. Give us a call right away at the number below, and we can send somebody to your house to resolve your asphalt issue right away."

A simple video along those lines should be the first step of your plan. It's a necessity.

The other videos that you want to create should be about your primary services. This ties in well with the SEO strategy discussed previously. You want to make sure you have a page on your website for each one of the services that you provide.

The other very powerful piece of content that you should incorporate, but should be phase two, would be your frequently asked questions, or FAQ. Make a list of the questions that people tend to ask and create a little video about it.

A few examples include: What to do in the event of a pothole; what to do about cracks in your driveway; Why restripe your parking lot. Get creative!

This is common information to you, but the average consumer doesn't know. Creating a little video providing answers to these frequently asked questions makes for great video content for your YouTube channel, to be syndicated on your social media profiles, and/or uploaded to your blog on your website.

Sharing Your Message

Now that we know what types of videos we want to create and how to create them, what should we say? Should we have a script? Should we wing it?

You want to be natural, you want to be authentic, and you want to be real. Some people must have a script because they don't feel comfortable doing video outside of a scripted methodology.

But, if there is any way you can get in front of a camera and speak naturally like you would to a customer in person about your services, that's going to work best.

What to Say

Here is a simple script you can follow: "At Joe's Paving Company, we provide a full range of paving services (to the specific area, whatever area you're in, or whatever service this video is about)." Have a brief description of what you do in that area, and then, "If you're in need of this service in your area, we can help. Call our office today at 555-5555."

Let's do an example from another industry. Say you are an auto repair shop owner specializing in general repair or 4x4 services, your page might say:

"From Standard Interval Maintenance, to extensive repair, XYZ has you covered. Don't pay high dealership pricing for the same service XYZ can provide for a fraction of the cost, using the same OEM parts and Manufacturer suggested procedures to keep your vehicle running at its best! You don't want to sit around. You don't want to have to call 10 different companies. You just want to feel confident that who you call is going to get to you within a reasonable period of time.

We are going to resolve the issue and we are not going to overcharge you. We can help you build an off-road machine capable of finding the road less traveled and exploring roads the average 4-wheel drive vehicle isn't capable of reaching. You can reach us at 555-5555. As a matter of fact, if you reference this coupon code "Auto Repair Video" we'll knock $20.00 off your repair."

A simple video like that for each one of your services should always include a call to action telling them what to do. Also, if you feel comfortable with it, referencing a discount could go a long way.

Don't over think this. Think about the core services that you offer. Shoot a quick 30-second to one-and-a-half-minute video about each and you're ready to roll.

What to Do with Your Video Content

What are you going to do with the videos once you've got them? Now that you have completed shooting your videos, what you want to do is setup a YouTube channel.

You can do this by going to YouTube.com. You want to upload your video, name it correctly and intelligently, putting it in terms that people will use when they're searching. If somebody is looking for auto repair services, they are going to type in "your city auto repair services." You want to name the video using your keywords.

When you upload it to YouTube, you want to title it "Denver Auto Repair specialists" or "Denver Hail Damage Repair services" and then put a description with a link to your site. "Visit us online at yourcompany.com/haildamagerepair" and then include a description about what you do, briefly outlining what was said in your video.

YouTube Best Practices

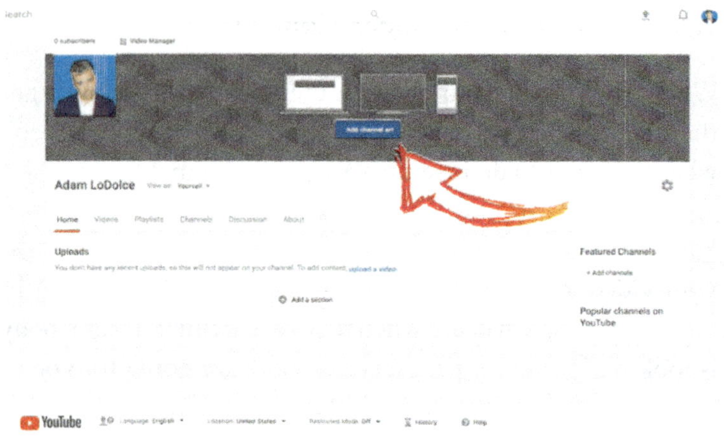

When you setup your channel, make sure that you give it a "city plus service, name of your company" title, instead of just your company name. You are also going to add tags with keywords to it. Don't just leave the tag area blank.

Make sure you use your name, address and phone number in every description on your YouTube channel because this is a good citation source.

As covered in the Google Maps optimization chapter, citation development is critical (having your company name, address and phone number referenced consistently across the web). This is a great place to get citations. Also, make sure that there's an image avatar with your company logo. You can update the default image by putting in your logo or put a picture of the team or office.

Here's some visual representation of this. If you log into

YouTube and create your channel, you'll get an email confirmation. Once you're set up, you can go to the "My Channel" settings and make some of the updates I referenced on the previous slide.

To change your logo, simply click "change" and choose your image–a very simple step.

Where it says "Your company name," it's going to default to something basic such as your email address on Google. You can hit "change" and update it to say "your city dentist" or "your city Auto repair services" and then a dash and your company name.

This gives you the chance to get your YouTube channel itself to show up for your keywords in the search engine. You will also have the opportunity to add your channel keywords. That is where you can type in words such as "your city driveway paving," "your city parking lot paving," "your city sealcoating," and of course your company name.

From there, there's a section where you can click "About your company" and put a description about who you are, what you do, and what areas you serve. You can get as creative with this area as you want, but it is most important to make sure you first put a description of your services, and your city.

If you're in Tampa, you put Tampa. If you're in Lakeland, you put Lakeland. If you're in Los Angeles, you put Los Angeles. Put your phone number and, again, restate your name, address and phone number. Citations are important. Having this in the description area is a powerful citation source.

Always put your name, address and phone number the same way as you did on your Google Map listing, your Angie's List listing, etc. That way, you will be consistent across the web, improving the probability of ranking in the Google Map listings.

Video Tagging Best Practices

Now, let's talk about video tagging best practices. Let's say you created the inventory of videos I recommended: an intro video and clips for each of your services.

How did you tag those videos to maximize the opportunity and to make sure you're going to rank well in search?

- Title Video with City Service - Company (always mix this up a little)
- Description should always start with http://url.com and then describe the service using those same keywords. ALWAYS ADD N.A.P. (Name, Address, Phone) INFO AT THE BOTTOM OF THE DESCRIPTION
- Use your keywords as tags and include the company name
- Choose most appropriate screenshot
- Click "advanced settings" and add address to video

The first thing you want to do is have your primary keywords in the title of the video as well as a description that includes the "http://" before your web address.

In the description area, you can put in "We're a full service XYZ company. We serve this area. This is our name, address and phone number," but at the very top, you should have your website address, including the "http://".

If you just put www.yourcompany.com, YouTube won't understand the link and it will show that it isn't clickable. If you put "http://" the link will be clickable, and visitors will go straight to your page, and they also get the link authority from having that link back to your website.

Choose the screenshot and add video. Whenever you upload your video you are able to control your title and your description, as well as the ability to add tags.

Titles Matter

Again, don't call your videos "your company name." Don't call it "teeth cleaning." Don't call it "auto repair." Call it "Your city + that service," and then your company name. Title your videos the same way that somebody would search.

If it's your intro video, you might want to call it "your city + your primary service" Example: you're a local "Lakeland cosmetic dentistry – XYZ Dentistry." If it's the teeth cleaning page, "your city teeth cleaning services – XYZ Dentistry".

It is really critical that you have the right titles on your video. This is what is going to make it so Google can locate it and include it in search results.

The next thing you want to do in your description is to put the link at the very top. The first thing you want to do is include a link back to the home page or to the specific page that you're discussing in the video.

If it's the teeth cleaning page, don't put a link to your home page. Put a link to that teeth cleaning page, and again "http://yourc ompany.com" — make sure you've got that "http://".

Below, you add your tags. Within those tags you can put in your city dentist, your city auto repairing, your city teeth cleaning, and everything in between.

What Else Can You Do with Your Videos?

Now that you've updated your video and you've properly optimized it, your title is correct, and your description is posted, how can we use these videos? Where are we going to leverage them? Well, to really get the benefits of that conversion component, we need those videos to be posted on our website and social profiles as well.

The best way to do this is to copy the "embed code" and post the videos right on your site. The intro video should be embedded on the home page and the service-specific videos should be posted on the appropriate subpages. The way we do this is right within our YouTube channel or YouTube account.

Go to the video manager and find the list of all the videos that you have. Choose the video that you want to post on your website and choose the share and embed option.

You will then be provided with this little piece of code, and that's what I have highlighted on the screen. It goes from I-frame to I-frame. This is the specific code for that video. If you are updating your website on your own, copy and paste the code right into your website's HTML. If you have a detached web manager, send the code off to them with details on where you want it posted.

Once the code is embedded in your HTML, it will show up on the page itself. That's what we really want to do with these videos. And, of course we don't have to limit ourselves to YouTube. There are a lot of very well known video sharing sites out there.

11

Email Marketing

Ever since there's been email, there's been email marketing. Email marketing is one of the oldest forms of advertising your business on the Internet.

Although it gets a bad rap because of all the spam going around, it's still one of the most effective forms of marketing.

I am a big believer in email marketing. It's a powerful way to get instant traffic to your website and getting the telephone to ring, but there is a right way and a wrong way to use it.

Did you know the easiest customer to sell to is the customer you already have?

Every self-proclaimed marketing expert will tell you that's nothing new. With that said, many paving business owners hardly ever market or keep in touch with their existing client base. Companies will spend thousands of dollars trying to get new customers but never think to market to the clients who already buy from them.

Why is that? I have a lot of ideas about this. I suspect business owners think that once a customer buys from them, they will just keep coming back on their own. Or maybe they simply don't want to bother their customers. The truth is customers want to hear from you and they want to be touched by your business. If you don't, your competition will.

How Do We Start an Email Marketing Campaign?

The first thing you need is an email marketing service. You shouldn't do this yourself for several reasons:

1. Your Internet Service Provider (ISP) will blacklist you for sending bulk mail.
2. You would have no stats for tracking your open emails
3. It would look unprofessional coming from your Microsoft Outlook box

With that said, let's take a look at some of the popular email marketing services, all of which are paid services and are priced based on the amount of emails you send.

Constant Contact

I have used Constant Contact in the past and I like it for several reasons. It has great tracking stats, the ability to post to your social networks and a relatively user-friendly interface.

Constant Contact has many templates available for use. You can also add your own custom templates. I think custom templates are a MUST for any business wanting to promote their brand. You will have to know a bit of HTML but if you don't, you can have a web designer create one for you at a fairly inexpensive cost.

MailChimp

Mailchimp is another service I have personally used and recommend. It's relatively easy to use and offers similar features to Constant Contact. The interface is clean and easy to use.

iContact

Personally, I have never used iContact, but after reading about it on their website www.icontact.com, it looks fairly intuitive and similar to both MailChimp and Constant Contact.

I think all of these services are a good solution for any business looking to add email marketing to its Internet marketing strategy.

How to Get Email Addresses

I am asked on a regular basis about how to get email addresses. It's not as easy as sending a letter in the USPS mail to anyone you want to. The reality of it is that just because they are your customer and you have their email address doesn't mean you can send them anything if you don't have their permission.

This certainly is a fine line, because you somehow already have their email address, and they have used your services before, so is it really considered spam? Technically, yes. You didn't ask them if you could send them specials or a newsletter in email form.

The first thing you really want to do is get your clients'

permission to add them to your email list. There are a variety of ways to do this, including placing a form on your website, putting a sign-up sheet on your counter or even a putting a space on your job ticket that they sign when you complete your service.

Explain that you send out tips about your industry or specials on a monthly basis and would love to have them on your mailing list. You might even offer a discount coupon off your services if they sign up.

Getting that email address is valuable, so if it cost you 5%, go for it. Remember, you want the opportunity to have your company's name in front of your customers every single month. You want to remain top-of-mind if one of their friends is looking for services like yours or if they run into an emergency.

I had a pest control service provider come to my home several years ago. He did a good job and was very professional.

Four or five years later, I needed the services of the company again. I lost his business card and could not remember the name of the company. I had to find another pest removal service. He lost the business because he never stayed in contact with me. It was a big job that he lost, $1,500.00 to be exact.

Start building your list today.

What to Send and How Often

First, what do I send? You must use the 80/20 rule, 80 percent good information and 20 percent sales. If all you send is emails about what services you offer, no one will ever read it. It's a great way to kill your list.

Draft up some information about your industry, give good homeowner tips, throw in some DIY tips, and make sure it's information that will help your customers. For the 20% sales, add a coupon or a special you are having, or offer something for your customers' friends and family.

How often you send your emails is very important. I always go with once per month, around the same time every month.

It is important to commit to a date. More than once a month is too much and annoys people.

I get an email from a company I purchased from in the past and get 3-4 emails a week from them, 100% sales, sometimes several times a day. I HATE IT and it drives me nuts. I removed myself from that list very quickly as I'm sure others have as well.

Get Legal

Make sure you have allowed customers the option to Opt Out of receiving email messages at the bottom of every message.

Make sure that it's easy because nothing is more annoying than receiving emails that you don't want. If someone does not want to receive your messages, then remove them from your list.

They may be getting emails from too many sources and just want to clean out their email box. It does not mean they will never buy from you again. But I will tell you this, if they want out and you keep sending email to them, it's a sure-fire way to bother them and they will likely never buy from you again.

Again, you want to leverage email marketing as part of your overall Internet marketing strategy. The best way to use it is to be sure you're collecting the email address from all your customers and prospects.

From there, use email marketing to get online reviews, engagement on your social media accounts and remain top-of-mind as a strategy to get more repeat and referral business.

What is the Best Time to Send an Email Campaign?

These general email send time tips are widely accepted by the email marketing community. They are great when you're starting off, but be sure to read on and see why they won't always work.

- Day-time vs. Night-time. While this one may be obvious, it's usually better to send out your email campaigns during the daytime. You know, when people are awake. Not asleep.

- Mad Mondays. The general consensus is that you should avoid sending out email blasts on Mondays. Why? People are already bummed out about the end of the weekend. They march into the office and are flooded with emails they've collected over the past few days. What's the first thing they do? Delete those emails of course!
- Weekends. Historically, weekends are the days when folks are out running errands and going on adventures. Weekends tend to have low open rates, so most marketers avoid them like the plague.
- Fan Favorites: Tuesday, Wednesday, and Thursday. Tuesday, Wednesday, and Thursday have traditionally been favorite days to send email campaigns, as email marketers seek to avoid the Monday angst and Friday's itchy feet. MailChimp confirms that Tuesday and Thursday are the two most popular days to send email newsletters.

12

PPC Strategy For Paving Companies

This is another subject that is broad and tough to tackle here, but we can outline a general approach that will be appropriate for any small business.

First, I want to talk about how we know all of this.

We monitor the top 200 markets in the US for four critical keywords:

- Paving company
- Paving contractor
- Driveway paving company
- Parking lot paving company

We know who is running ads, *what ads they are running,* and lots more.

Check out the information we have!

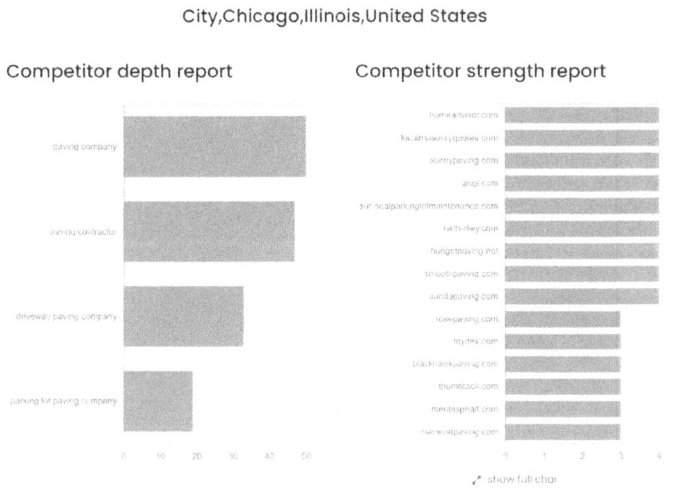

This summary shows who is running ads on those target keywords. Note that you see homeadvisor.com, angi.com, mydex.com, localmasonryquotes.com, and thumbtack.com on this report. **This is one of the biggest sources of leads for these companies who resell them.**

Now, look at how much individual, detailed information we have:

Advertiser	Keywords Count	Locations Count	Ads Count
3dbrickpaving.com	3	1	9
aandapaving.com	4	1	43
abenvironmentalcons.com	1	1	1
ablepavingandmasonry.com	1	1	1
accu-pavingcompany.com	3	1	78
acornasphaltmasonry.com	3	1	17
allriteblacktop.com	2	1	3
americanasphalt.net	3	1	51
angi.com	4	1	214
aplusbrickpaversllc.com	1	1	1
belrockinc.com	2	1	3
billdr.co	3	1	11
blackhawkpaving.com	3	1	91

These are the individual advertisers and examples of their ads.

The next few show snapshots of a summary report I generated about the market.

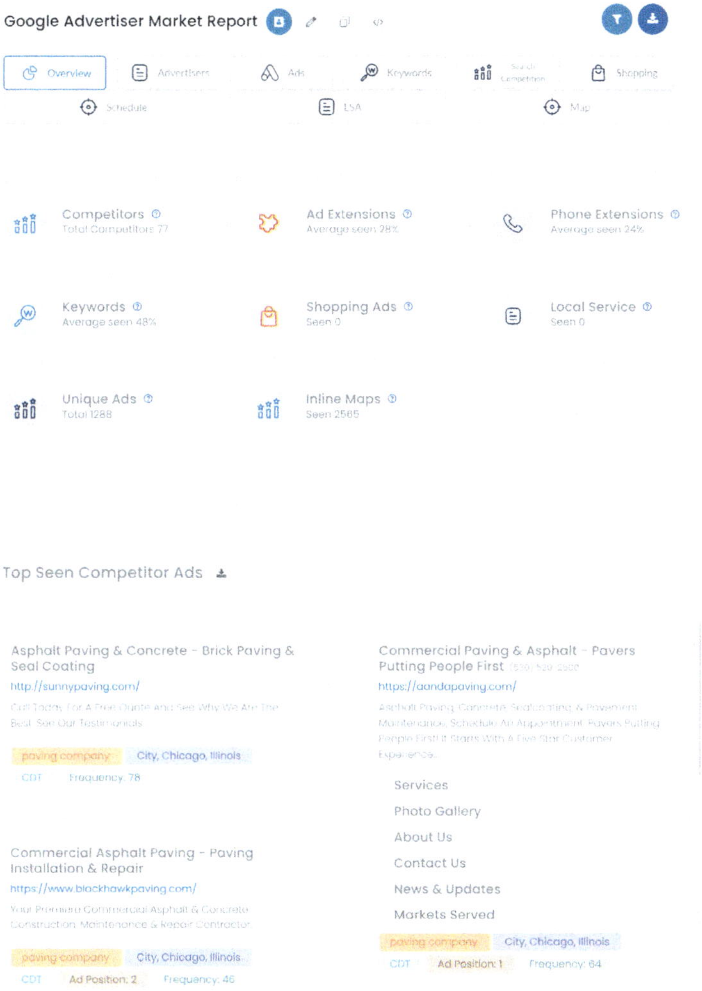
Google Advertiser Market Report
Overview
Advertisers
Ads
Keywords
Search Competition
Shopping
Schedule
LSA
Map
Competitors
Total Competitors 77
Ad Extensions
Average seen 28%
Phone Extensions
Average seen 24%
Keywords
Average seen 48%
Shopping Ads
Seen 0
Local Service
Seen 0
Unique Ads
Total 1288
Inline Maps
Seen 2585
Top Seen Competitor Ads
Asphalt Paving & Concrete - Brick Paving & Seal Coating
http://sunnypaving.com/
paving company
City, Chicago, Illinois
CDT
Frequency: 78
Commercial Asphalt Paving - Paving Installation & Repair
https://www.blackhawkpaving.com/
paving company
City, Chicago, Illinois
CDT
Ad Position: 2
Frequency: 46
Commercial Paving & Asphalt - Pavers Putting People First
https://aandapaving.com/
Services
Photo Gallery
About Us
Contact Us
News & Updates
Markets Served
paving company
City, Chicago, Illinois
CDT
Ad Position: 1
Frequency: 64

Search Term Competition

Export CSV

Search Term	Frequency	Ecomm	LSA	Map	Exter
paving company	1047	0	0	642	51.58
paving contractor	621	0	0	639	59.1
driveway paving company	625	0	0	642	53.92
parking lot paving company	142	0	0	642	26.06

1

Related Search Term

Export CSV

Search Item
paving companies chicago
asphalt paving company
rose paving lawsuit
paving company near me
commercial parking lot paving
parking lot paving companies near me
paving company meaning
rose paving company
commercial paving contractors near me
driveway paving company near schaum
parking lot paving company near schaui
paving company near schaumburg, il
driveway paving company near chicago
driveway paving contractors near me

Note that these are the actual keywords that are used to trigger these ads, and how frequently they are used.

HINT HINT you should be using these keywords in your own Google Ads campaigns (changing out the locations, of course).

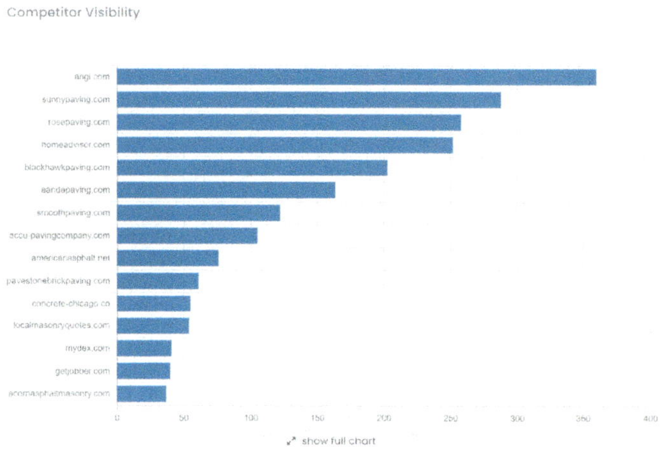

Competitors

Export CSV

Advertisers name	Visibility	Unique ads	Shopping	LSA	Map	Extension %	Phone %
angi.com	360	214	-	-	-	59.72	0
sunnypaving.com	288	82	-	-	-	37.85	0
rosepaving.com	258	135	-	-	-	61.24	69.77
homeadvisor.com	252	158	-	-	-	62.7	0
blackhawkpaving.com	203	87	-	-	-	20.2	1.97
aandapaving.com	164	29	-	-	-	93.9	96.34
smoothpaving.com	122	40	-	-	-	72.13	98.36
accu-pavingcompany.com	105	75	-	-	-	55.24	56.19
americanasphalt.net	76	57	-	-	-	82.89	59.21
pavestonebrickpaving.com	61	12	-	-	-	60.66	100
concrete-chicago.co	55	28	-	-	-	70.91	0
localmasonryquotes.com	54	31	-	-	-	27.78	48.15
mydex.com	41	31	-	-	-	46.34	70.73
getjobber.com	40	22	-	-	-	65	0
acornasphaltmasonry.com	37	16	-	-	-	72.97	97.3

If you want to learn about your market, give us a call and we can provide a similar report for you.

The Two Main PPC Platforms

There are really two main players in the Pay Per Click space – Google, and Bing. Google has the vast majority of the market share, while Bing also serves ads on Yahoo and AOL Search (yes, it still exists!).

We recommend ignoring Bing as you get started. You are going to want to test things in Google, get them working right, and show that you can run ads profitably there. Then, you can simply import what is working into Bing. They are no fools, and they make it very easy for you to do that.

Some people will include Facebook in the PPC category and it is true, that is one of the payment models they have. The more common way to categorize these channels is "Search Engine Marketing" (SEM) and "Social Media Marketing" (SMM) and SEM is typically the one people have in mind when they say PPC.

We are going to focus now on Google Ads and restrict our discussion to them, as they are the most common ads and the ones you are going to want to do.

Types Of Google Ads

There are several different types of ads you can run on Google's networks.

Search ads – these are the ones that you probably think of when you think of "Google Ads." They are based on keyword searches and are associated with a Cost Per Click (CPC).

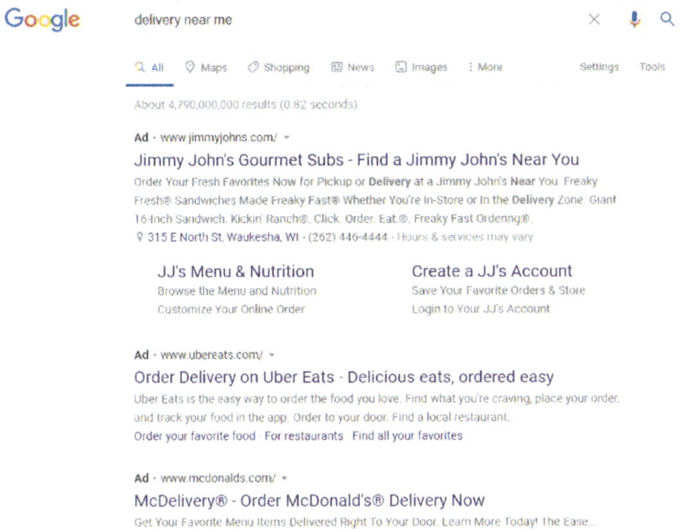

Display ads – these are the ads you see when browsing websites. There are really two main campaign types here.

Display network campaigns targeting people who visit specific websites or have different interests.

Retargeting campaigns that serve ads to people who visited your website.

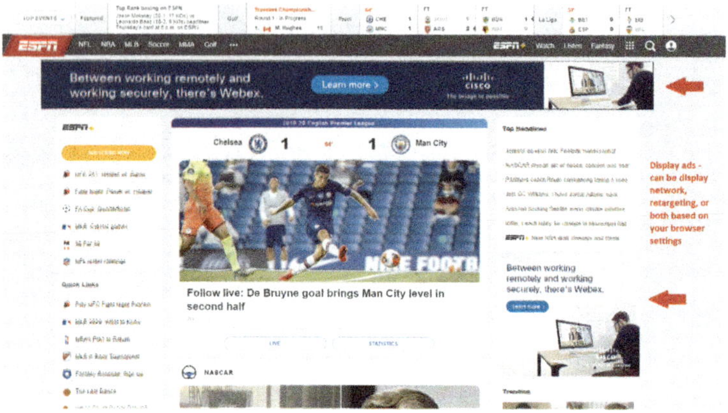

There is another, newer type of display ad called "discovery ads" that Google recently rolled out to try to compete with Facebook's display reach. We will not cover those here.

Video ads – these are video-based ads that primarily run on YouTube. These are a bit more advanced and typically will not be a good fit for most paving businesses, and so we will not cover them here.

There are a few other ad types – like Shopping ads – which are a bit advanced and not a good fit for most paving businesses and we will skip those.

What Campaigns Paving Companies Should Run

There are two types of Google Ads campaigns we would advise all paving business owners to consider running: search ads and retargeting ads.

For the search ads, there are a few things to keep in mind.

You should have a high-converting landing page to send the traffic to. Do not send paid traffic to your home page. You should consider implementing call tracking (check out Call Rail) on those landing pages to help measure the kinds of leads the ads are bringing in.

Do not advertise outside of your service area. You can avoid this by geofencing the area you want to show ads during the campaign setup. This means to restrict where the ads show to the location where you will accept jobs.

You should have Google Analytics set up on your website, and should also have conversion tracking in place so that you can measure the results and what your return on investment is.

If you are going to advertise multiple services, you are going to need a different landing page for each one. The reason for this is Quality Score. This is how Google scores ad bid and rewards those it thinks will serve the best experience to clickers. That score depends on how well your ad text and landing page match up to the keyword the searcher clicked to get there. If you have a high quality score, you will be rewarded with lower Cost Per Click.

The most important thing about search ads is this: know your numbers. You need to know what your acceptable cost per acquisition is – if you can afford to pay $100 for each new customer and be profitable, then you better be sure you are not paying $150!

For your retargeting campaign, you just have to get the images made and fire it up – it's relatively simple to set up and since you'll be showing ads to people who visited your website, there is not a lot of complicated setup here.

There are a lot of little steps to setting up these campaigns and there are a lot of guide out there that can show you how to do that, so we won't use the space here to do so. However, we do want to show you an easy way to find the right keywords to start advertising with.

Keyword Research

If you have not done so already go ahead and set up your Google Ads account. We recommend using the same Gmail address you used to set up your Google Business Profile account.

Once you have that set up and you are in there, go to the "Tools" area and navigate to the Keyword Planner. It should look something like this:

Remember the categories you picked when you set up your Google Business Profile? You are going to use that list here to find what keywords Google thinks is relevant to you. Start with your primary category – enter it in the search box there and click "Get Results."

In this example I am going to use "paving contractors."

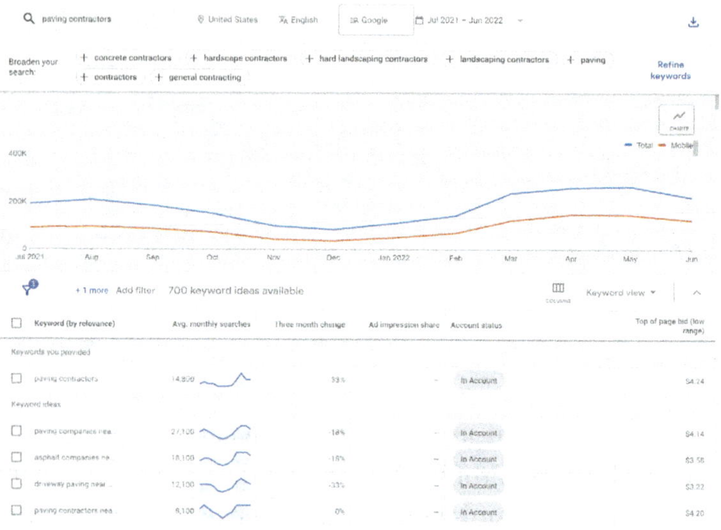

You can see that you get a ton of useful data here. Keep in mind that you are looking at data for the entire US, and that is ok. Remember that you are going to geofence your campaign to your service area.

Take a look at the "Top of page bid" estimates to get a sense of what you're going to need to be spending per click in order to be competitive. If you have everything set up well (high-converting landing page, great quality scores, etc) you can expect a conversion rate in the range of 5-10%. It can be higher or lower depending on the business type, but it is a good rule of thumb. Use those numbers as a sanity check on the bid prices here. Just because Google says that is what the bids should be does not mean you have to use them. You might find you can get away with bidding less in your geofenced area, and in fact you often can.

I would suggest downloading the keyword ideas and saving them.

The next thing you want to do is add your city modifier and see what happens. Here, I'll use Dallas.

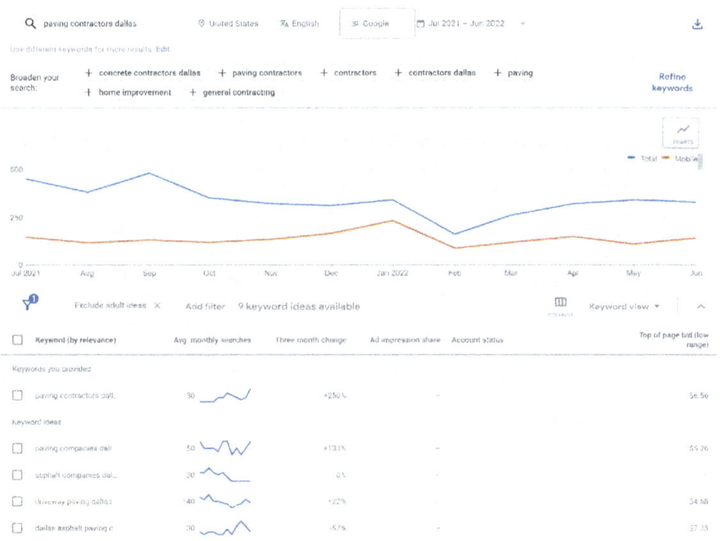

Notice the graph looks different – that's because (as you probably know) the paving season in Dallas is not the same as the average paving season that includes the north.

You are going to get a set of geo-modified keywords. Download those too. Repeat this for each major city in your service area that you do business in.

Now, repeat all of these steps for your other categories.

You are going to have a ton of useful information that will guide you in what to do next. At minimum, you are going to need a dedicated landing page for each service you want to run ads for. You can even make service + city landing pages if you want to get super-detailed and get the best possible quality scores.

Then, you are going to want to build search campaigns for each service type, with ad groups for each related sub-group of keywords. You can even do single-keyword-ad-groups (SKAGs) – which is the approach we prefer.

If you are new to Google Ads, or even trying it again – we suggest picking one key service and starting with that. Build your landing page, make sure all of the tracking is set up correctly, build and run the campaigns, and see if it's producing profitable leads for you. Once you have that first campaign working for you go ahead and import it into Bing.

Then, do the same thing for the next service you want to advertise.

It can be a lot of work, but it is a tried and true way to generate leads for a paving company!

13

Measure Your Success

Congratulations! Now That You Have...

- Built and optimized your website
- An ongoing link building strategy in place where you're creating inbound links and moving up in the search engines
- Implemented email marketing and social media marketing initiatives, and
- Possibly implemented a paid online marketing campaign including Pay-Per-Click and Pay-Per-Lead services...

...You need to put some tools in place so that you can track, measure and quantify your data to ensure that you're moving in a positive direction.

Analytics Tracking

There are a lot of different tracking mechanisms that you can put in place. I'm going to recommend three core tracking mechanisms:

- Google Analytics
- Keyword Tracking
- Call Tracking

The first is Google Analytics. Google Analytics is a great website data analysis tool and it's completely free. Google Analytics will show you specifically:

- How many visitors got to your website on a daily, weekly, monthly, and annual basis
- What keywords they typed in to get there
- What pages on your website they visited
- How long they stayed

The main thing you want to see from Google Analytics is where you started and where you are now.

You want to ask yourself: When I started this whole Internet marketing process, how many visitors was I getting to my website? Maybe it was 5, 20, 100, or 500, but it's good to know. Then you can compare to future data on an ongoing basis.

Ultimately, what you are looking for is whether or not the number of visitors to your website is increasing. Is the variety of keywords that they're finding you with increasing? Are you moving in a positive direction?

You can also set up reports within Google Analytics. To get set up on Google Analytics, you just go to Google.com/analytics. It's a simple process. You verify that you own the website through a variety of different methods, and then install a small piece of code into your website's HTML. After you have done that, you've got the tracking in place and are ready to go.

Sample Google Analytics Traffic Reports

Traffic Overview:

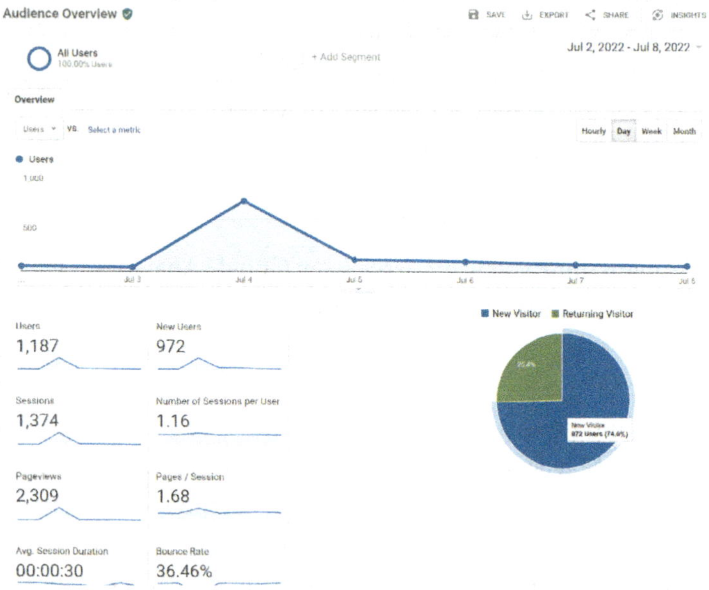
Audience Overview
SAVE
EXPORT
SHARE
INSIGHTS
All Users
100.00% Users
+ Add Segment
Jul 2, 2022 - Jul 8, 2022
Overview
Users
VS.
Select a metric
Hourly
Day
Week
Month
Users
1,000
500
Jul 3
Jul 4
Jul 5
Jul 6
Jul 7
Jul 8
New Visitor
Returning Visitor
Users
1,187
New Users
972
Sessions
1,374
Number of Sessions per User
1.16
Pageviews
2,309
Pages / Session
1.68
Avg. Session Duration
00:00:30
Bounce Rate
36.46%

Keyword Tracking

The other tracking mechanism that I recommend is keyword tracking.

At the beginning of this process, we talked about keyword research to determine what keywords people are typing in when they need your services.

We came up with a list and all those keywords were combined with your cities and sub-cities.

There are tools that will tell you how you're ranking on Google, Yahoo, and Bing for those various keywords. A few options include:

- Bright Local
- White Spark
- Raven Tools
- WebCEO

The keyword tracking tool I recommend is called BrightLocal.

You can learn more about it at www.brightlocal.com. There is a cost associated with this service, but it is great resource for tracking your search engine optimization progress.

You take your keywords, put them into the BrightLocal Keyword Tracker and then set up a weekly and monthly report that shows where you rank on Google, Yahoo and Bing for your most important keywords.

With a report like this, you can easily see how your website is trending in the search engines.

You'll see yourself move up in the results if you've built out the website correctly with the right on-page factors (title tags, H1 tags, meta descriptions, etc.), if you're building links, developing citations and have a proactive review acquisition system in place.

If you see yourself stagnating, you can go back to that keyword, figure out which page is optimized for it, look at your links and link profile, and whatever is necessary to push that keyword to the next level.

Call Tracking

The third really important tracking mechanism that I recommend is call tracking. Having better rankings and more visits to your website is all fine and dandy, but in most businesses, nothing happens until a call is made.

Calls are crucial to your business. You want to have some type of tracking mechanism in place to know how many calls are coming in on a monthly basis and what's happening within those conversations.

Are calls turning into sales? That's where the rubber meets the road. That's why we're doing all of this. Who cares if you're in the number one position if it doesn't result in dollars to the business?

There are several call tracking tools that you can use. Here are a few:

- CallRail
- WhatConverts

Most of these call tracking services will let you choose a phone number based on your area code. So, you type in the number you want to get. It's a nominal fee on a monthly basis ($2 - $5 per month), and you get a tracking number.

Then, you can take that tracking phone number and you can put it on the graphics on your website so that you can track the number of calls and even listen to recordings of the conversation.

That number will be set to ring in your office. It's just a forwarding number. If somebody dials it, it still rings to your office like always, but it is a tracking number.

You can report on the number of calls using the Internet and play back recordings of those conversations. It's extremely powerful to know the number of calls you were getting when you started versus the number after you incorporated your new marketing strategy.

You can go in and listen to those conversations and ascertain how many of those calls turned into booked service while knowing what the revenue associated with that service is. That is how you get a true gauge on the return on investment associated with your online marketing strategy.

These are the types of tracking mechanisms I recommend. There are a lot of different things you can do, but having analytics, keyword tracking, and call tracking really gives you the most important key performance indicators to gauge your progress.

14

Final Thoughts

If you have been implementing these things as you have gone through the book you should be in great shape now. You already should be seeing more leads and new customers from your efforts. Nice work!

If you are not there yet that is OK too. Pick the area you feel most comfortable tackling first and go from there. Depending on how much of this you have set up already (or have not set up) it might seem like a daunting task to wrap your arms around.

You may have read this book and concluded that you do not want to do any of this yourself. If that is the case, and you would like to consider working with us, here is what I would like you to do.

Go to https://pavingmarketers.com/book and schedule a call with me.

Here is what we are going to do for you:

Keyword Research – we are going to take a look at your business and put together a keyword list for you. We are also going to take a look at where you are ranking currently for those terms. This will help us figure out where you are at and what could use some improvement.

Conversion – we are going to take a look at your website and give you feedback on how it is set up. Will it work as is or does it need to be revised?

Authority – how are you doing with respect to your competitors? Are their sites much "stronger" than yours is? Can you compete effectively? How are you doing with reviews?

Plan of Action – we are going to recommend a course of action – what needs to be done based on where you are today to potentially double, triple, or 10x your sales over the next six to nine months.

Now, my time is valuable, and so is my team's. If someone asked us to put this report together for them, we would charge $349 for it. The value you can get from this information is far greater than that.

Frankly, at that price it is a steal.

However, you have made the commitment to invest time in reading my book and I appreciate that. Chances are if you are reading this part you have read the rest of it.

So, I am including a surprise bonus here – we will do this

assessment for you for free as a thanks for doing that, subject to two commitments:

- If my team and I take the time to do this assessment for you, that you will show up for the call.
- If what we show you is compelling, you're serious about potentially hiring us to do this for you and take your internet marketing strategy and run it on your behalf, as we've done for hundreds of other clients.

If that sounds good to you, and you'd like to take us up on that, head over to https://pavingmarketers.com/book and schedule that call with me!